DESIGNER'S SHOWCASE Vol.03   Akihito Fumita   文田昭仁

CONTENTS

4 INTRODUCTION

PROJECTS

Showroom
6 NISSAN GALLERY GLOBAL HEADQUARTERS
日産グローバル本社ギャラリー

Showroom
22 NISSAN GALLERY GINZA
日産銀座ギャラリー

Showroom
36 NISSAN GALLERY HEADQUARTERS (old)
日産本社ギャラリー（旧本社）

Showroom
42 NISSAN GALLERY SAPPORO
日産札幌ギャラリー

Guest Hall
48 NISSAN GRANDRIVE
日産グランドライブ

Motorshow Booth
54 THE 35TH TOKYO MOTOR SHOW NISSAN BOOTH
第35回東京モーターショー　日産ブース

Motorshow Booth
62 THE 36TH TOKYO MOTOR SHOW NISSAN BOOTH
第36回東京モーターショー　日産ブース

Motorshow Booth
66 THE 37TH TOKYO MOTOR SHOW NISSAN BOOTH
第37回東京モーターショー　日産ブース

70 INTERVIEW 1

Hand Relaxation
72 NATURAL BODY NAMBA CITY
ナチュラルボディ　なんばCITY店

Hand Relaxation
74 NATURAL BODY KOBE INTERNATIONAL HOUSE SOL
ナチュラルボディ　神戸国際会館 SOL店

Hand Relaxation
76 NATURAL BODY SHIBUYA PARCO PART 3
ナチュラルボディ　渋谷 PARCO PART 3店

Hand Relaxation
80 NATURAL BODY HANKYU INTERNATIONAL
ナチュラルボディ　阪急インターナショナル店

Boutique
84 M,I,D, SHOP UMEDA HANKYU
エム・アイ・ディーショップ　阪急うめだ店

Boutique
88 M,I,D, SHOP YURAKUCHO HANKYU
エム・アイ・ディーショップ　有楽町阪急店

Pressroom
90 M,I,D, PRESS ROOM
エム・アイ・ディー プレスルーム

Office
94 M,I,D, HEADQUARTERS
エム・アイ・ディー本社

Office
96 M,I,D, HEADQUARTERS ANNEX
エム・アイ・ディー本社アネックス

Boutique
98 M-PREMIER SHIJOKAWARAMACHI HANKYU STORE
エム・プルミエ　四条河原町阪急店

Boutique
100 M-PREMIER TENMAYA HIROSHIMA HACCHOBORI STORE
エム・プルミエ　天満屋広島八丁堀店

Boutique
102 TRE PINI
トレピニ

Accessory Shop
104 ETE AOYAMA
エテ　青山本店

Accessory Shop
106 ETE＋ NAGOYA LACHIC
エテ・プラス　名古屋ラシック店

Boutique
108 THE SUPER SUITS STORE AWAJICHO
ザ・スーパースーツストア　淡路町店

Boutique & Common Space
110 OSAKA TAKASHIMAYA ROOM IN BLOOM
ルームインブルーム 大阪髙島屋

112 INTERVIEW 2

Showroom
114 SPIRITUAL MODE MINAMIAOYAMA
スピリチュアルモード　南青山

Showroom
122 SPIRITUAL MODE KYOTO
スピリチュアルモード　京都

Showroom
128 DCMX SITE
DCMX サイト

Hair Salon
132 K-TWO UMEDA
ケイ・ツー　梅田店

Hair Salon
134 K-TWO SHINSAIBASHI
ケイ・ツー　心斎橋店

Hair Salon
138 SALON
サロン

Boutique
140 ANAYI SHINJUKU ISETAN
アナイ　新宿伊勢丹店

Boutique
142 ANAYI HIROSHIMA FUKUYA EKIMAE
アナイ　福屋広島駅前店

Boutique
144 ESSENCE OF ANAYI TOKYO MIDTOWN
エッセンス オブ アナイ　東京ミッドタウン店

Boutique
146 ANAYI NISHINOMIYA HANKYU
アナイ　西宮阪急店

Boutique
148 MANOUQUA SHIN MARUNOUCHI BUILDING
マヌーカ 新丸ビル店

Lifestyle Shop
150 IXC COLLECTA TAMAGAWA TAKASHIMAYA
イクスシー コレクタ　玉川髙島屋店

Boutique
152 INHALE + EXHALE KOBE FASHION MART
インヘイル+エクスヘイル　神戸ファッションマート店

Boutique
154 INHALE + EXHALE SHINKOBE ORIENTAL HOTEL
インヘイル+エクスヘイル　新神戸オリエンタルホテル店

156 INTERVIEW 3

Office
158 FUMITA DESIGN OFFICE
文田昭仁デザインオフィス

Office Exterior
162 LITTLE ANDERSEN
リトルアンデルセン

House
164 H-HOUSE
H邸

PRODUCT

Exhibition
170 Tokyo Designers Block 2001
東京デザイナーズブロック 2001

Exhibition
171 Tokyo Designers Block 2003
東京デザイナーズブロック 2003

Bathtub
172 BEIGNET
ベニエ

Accessory
173 EMF Collection
EMF コレクション

Vase
174 nest
ネスト

Vase
174 face
フェイス

Aroma Pot
175 pebble
ペブル

176 DETAIL DESCRIPTION
作品解説

INTRODUCTION

Essay on Akihito Fumita

文田昭仁論

By Masaaki Takahashi
文 高橋正明

その作品にはどれも独自のクールさが漂い、完結した世界観がうかがえる。さほど遠くない近未来にあるようなインナー・ランドスケープが広がり、機械美礼賛を静かに謳うメカニックで蠱惑的な抽象のエレメントやディテールが次々に見る者の視界に現れ、空間を分節していく。この世界の設計者は文田昭仁。光さえもまるでマテリアルと化してしまうかのような建築的で造形力のあるインテリアは、彼ならではの世界だ。商業施設のインテリアデザイナーとして日本を代表する者を選ぶとすれば、今、彼の名を外すことは不可能であろう。文田の作品といえば、日産自動車の一連のショールームなど（P.6〜69）を任されていることが知られている。また、カッティングエッジで、どこかメタリックなイメージの尖ったものばかりではなく、木を効果的に使った温かみのある作品があることも知っておいて良いだろう。

文田昭仁のデザインをみると、インテリアデザイナーとアーキテクトの両方の手法を融合させ、いくぶんか後者に寄りながら、独自の観点で空間を立ち上げていることが分かる（学生時代には磯崎新やチャールズ・ジェンクスの建築書や言語にも影響されたという）。インテリアデザイナーの手法とは、与えられた空間を空箱として捉え、その中を加減的なプラス／マイナス計算と手続きで整えることだ。空間の条件そのものに対しては、意図するかしないかは別にしても触れることは控える。条件を固定することは、必ずしも有利に働くとは限らないが、制限をあえてそのままにすることが創意を実現するのに都合がよい枠組みを与えることもある。そのレベル上でのクリエーションこそがインテリアデザイナーの見せ場となる。これらは言わば、内から外へとズームアウトしていくようなミクロから入る作業である。

これに対してアーキテクト的アプローチはマクロ的で、空間を分析することから始まり、ボリュームの在り方を捉え直していく。諸条件を構想の中で足場として渡し、三次元の中で加減だけでなく乗除も使う切り口を考えながらロジックを組み立てる。

文田は天井を、壁を、床を当たり前の定義から切り離し、「無記名」のものに還元することから始める。物件を、その空間を、いま一度全体を抽象化して検証するという一見遠回りな過程にくぐらせる。このプロセスは非常に建築的な、しかも高度に抽象的なコンセプトメークを思わせる。試みに、ある作品、例えば、システムバスのショールーム「スピリチュアル・モード」（P.116〜129）の画像をシャッフルし、テーブル上にランダムに配置して眺めてみよう。それぞれは抽象画にも似ているが、仮に平面が立面であっても、立面が平面であっても違和感がないようにも見える。あるいは、天井が床に、床が壁に置き換わったとしても成立し得るようなシーンが構成されていることに気付くだろう。更にそこに置かれた文田自身のデザインによるドーナツ型のバスタブまでもがインテリアの要素としてどの位置にどういうかたちで置かれても全く違和感がない。

彼はただステージをつくり、空間を構成するだけではなく、その中に、これも自らがデザインした無数のオリジナル・プレイヤー（演者）を配し、役を演じさせるコレオグラファー（演出家）でもあるのだ。彼がインテリアのための照明やソファやチェアなど家具、造作、装飾のためでもあるオブジェ、高級バスタブなどにみるようにプロダクトデザインの完成度は非常に高い。こうして、ディテールの一つに至るまですべてがフェティッシュなまでのこだわりのもとに設えられ、さまざまな装置や仕掛けが巧妙に織り込まれ、全体が共鳴して、一つの世界観が実現される。そこには職人的な、技術者的なセンスや素材への思いが表出され、そのミクロとマクロのバランス感覚は絶妙である。

文田デザインを語る時には、その特徴的な、そしてしばしばエクスペリメンタルな光の演出にもふれておかなくてはならないだろう。それは確かに照明器具を用いることには違いないのだが、空間全体を光で包み、あるいは、例えばブティックの「ANAYI」（P.140〜145）に見るように、木の造作を照らし、またそれに線状に沿ったり、個々の部分から計算されたかたちで漏れたりすることで、マテリアルのように配置されている。造作のパーツはあたかも空中に浮遊し、しかもある一定の方向に動きつつ、そのまま時間が停止したかのようだ。浮遊感といえば、「エム・アイ・ディー・プレスルーム」（P.90）の炉心棒を思わせる蛍光ランプが貫入したガラス面もそうだ。時間と空間とは実は不可分に一体であるという宇宙的原理を想起させてくれる素晴らしいコンセプトが具現化されている。これらのインテリアは全体がアート・インスタレーションとして設定された空間のようにさえ見える。

文田は、これまで感性という言葉には距離を取ってきたと言うが、近年はそうした部分にも心動かされる自分を感じている。たとえば物語の文章の一節でも、その文章の背後から立ち上がる感性的なもの、感覚的なものに注意を向けるようになった。デザインといい造形というが、その根源は視覚や計算を超えた、感性を総動員する認知的＝身体的レベルでの共振かもしれない。彼のデザインの中にそうした要素が取り込まれる日が来るのは、そう先のことではないだろう。

たかはし・まさあき
デザイン批評。オランダのインテリア誌 Frame、建築誌 Mark など、海外の雑誌に、日本の建築、デザイン、アートについて寄稿。編集プロダクション「ブライズヘッド」主宰。社会と建築をつなぐ団体 SHA-ken（www.sha-ken.org）主催。著書「建築プレゼンの掟」「次世代の空間デザイン21名の仕事」「Design City Tokyo」「商店建築増刊 ワールド・ハイパー・インテリア vol.1〜3」他多数。DIESEL DENIM GALLERY AOYAMA のキュレーターも務めている。www.brizhead.jp

A characteristic coolness hangs in the air in every one of his works, letting the viewer visit a complete worldview. An inner landscape that exists in a not-so-far-off future spreads out before the viewer, as mechanical, dazzling, abstract elements and details that quietly advocate machine beauty enter his field of vision one after another, articulating the space. This world's designer is Akihito Fumita. These skillfully crafted, architectural interiors in which light itself is transformed into a design material could only have been created by him. When it comes time to choose a commercial interior designer who represents Japan, his name cannot be left out. Well-known among Fumita's works is a series of facilities ranging from showrooms entrusted to him by Nissan Motor Co. I suppose it should also be known that his creations are not all sharp, cutting-edge works with a metallic-image; he also has warm works in which he used wood effectively.

Akihito Fumita's designs combine the techniques of an interior designer with those of an architect, and while to a certain extent he emphasizes the latter, we can see that he is building spaces from his original point of view. (In his student days he is said to have been influenced by the architectural books and language of Arata Isozaki and Charles Jencks.) As for interior designer techniques, he regards a space as an empty box, and prepares by calculating its positives and negatives. The requirements of the space force him to hold off on his design, whether he wants to or not. Fixed requirements do not always work to your advantage, but sometimes daring to accept limits provides a helpful framework for expressing an original idea. Creation from that standpoint becomes the high point for the designer. This is work begun from the micro level, in which you zoom out from the interior to the exterior, so to speak.

In contrast with this, the architectural approach is macro, beginning with analyzing the space and then realigning your perceptions of what the structure taken as a whole should be. When you traverse various conditions as footholds in your planning, you think of not just addition and subtraction, but also multiplication and division, as openings in the three dimensions as you develop your logic.

Fumita begins by cutting loose from the obvious definitions of ceiling, walls and floor and returning to a space without preconceptions. He puts the space through the seemingly roundabout process of first observing it abstractly. This process recalls extremely architectural and furthermore highly abstract conceptualization. As an experiment, what if we took the images from a given work, for example the system-bath showroom "Spiritual Mode" (pp.114, 122), shuffled them, and randomly placed them on a table top? They each would look like an abstract painting. But if a level-surface view were swapped with an elevational view or an elevational view with a level-surface view, they would not seem out of place. Or, if the ceiling were transposed for the floor, or the floor for a wall, I suppose we would realize that a conceivable scene was being put together. Furthermore, if we placed the donut-shaped bathtub designed by Fumita as an interior element in any position and in any form at all, there would be no sense whatsoever that it was out of place.

He does not merely create a stage and compose the space, but rather, he is the choreographer who places within it countless original players he designed himself, and makes them play their parts. As can be seen in the high-grade bath tub and elsewhere, the level of accomplishment of the product design of the objets d'art he uses as lighting, furniture, fixtures and ornaments in his interiors is exceedingly high. In this way, a single detail is implemented based on obsessiveness that goes to the point of fetish. Various devices and tricks are ingeniously interwoven. The whole resonates, and a single worldview is achieved. He expresses his artisanlike and engineerlike senses, along with his affection for the raw materials, and the resulting balance between micro and macro is miraculous.

In speaking about Fumita's designs, I suppose I also must touch on his characteristic and frequently experimental light productions. To be sure, he does use light fixtures. But in enveloping the overall space in light - or, for example, as seen in the boutique "Anayi (P.140-)," in using light to illuminate wooden fixtures, to follow their lines or to shine through in a form calculated based on their individual parts - he places light like a building material. It's as if a fixture's parts were suspended in midair and furthermore time was stopped while they were moving in a fixed direction.

While we're talking about the sensation of an object being suspended in midair, another example is the glass surface penetrated by a fluorescent lamp, reminiscent of a nuclear reactor core, in the "M,I,D, Press Room" (p.90). It is the embodiment of an excellent concept that reminds us of the physics principle that space and time are indivisibly one. These interiors, taken as a whole, even look like art installations.

Fumita says he has kept his distance from the word sensitivity, but in recent years he has felt himself become fascinated by that aspect. For example, when he reads part of a sentence in a story, he has begun turning his attention to the sensitivity, the sensibility, that stands behind that sentence.

Design is said to be good modeling, but its starting point may be a resonance beyond the visual or calculations, of the cognitive being equivalent to the physical, that mobilizes sensitivity. I doubt it will be long before that element begins to be incorporated into his designs.

Masaaki Takahashi
Masaaki Takahashi is an independent writer and the curator of DIESEL DENIM GALLERY AOYAMA. He contributes to foreign magazines including "Frame" and "Mark." Takahashi has established his own editorial production company, Brizhead. Book he has authored include "Japan The New Mix: Interiors", "Architecture and More", "Design City Tokyo", "World Hyper Interior vol.1～3", and more. www.brizhead.jp

NISSAN GALLERY GLOBAL HEAD QUARTERS

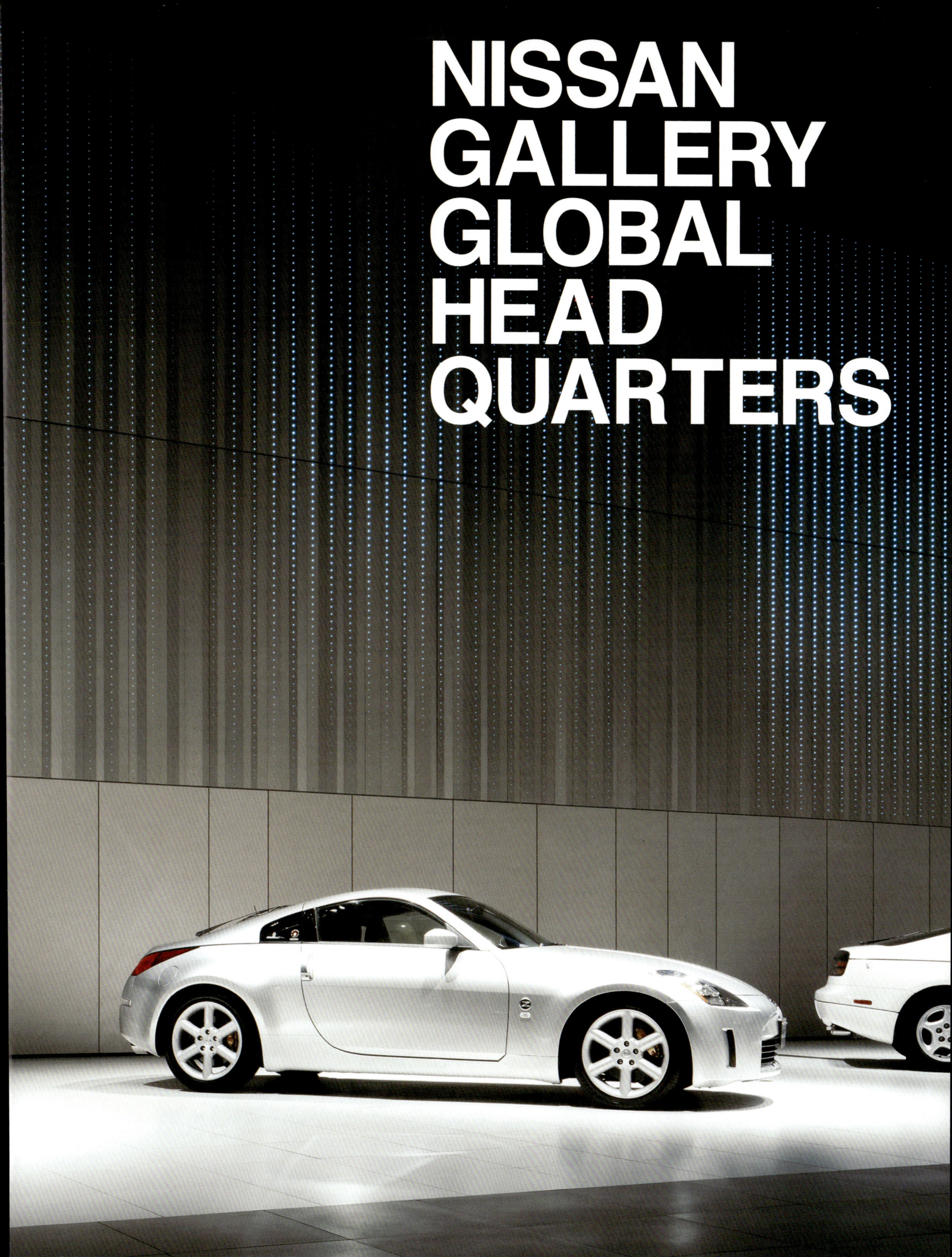

Showroom
**NISSAN GALLERY
GLOBAL HEADQUARTERS**
Minatomirai, Yokohama
日産グローバル本社ギャラリー
Completion : August 2009
Total area : 4500㎡

P.6・7　展示スペースLED壁を見る
P.8・9　LED壁を見る。
　　　　壁の一部は昇降式
P.6・7　The LEDs display wall
　　　　on the exhibition space.
P.8・9　The detail of the LEDs
　　　　display wall.

P.10 上　　LED壁のディテール
P.10 下　　2階通路から1階展示スペースを見下ろす
P.10・11　展示スペース
P.11 下　　2階通路から1階展示スペースを見下ろす
P.10 upper　The detail of the LEDs display wall.
P.10 lower　A look down at the exhibition space from the second floor.
P.10・11　The exhibition space.
P.11 lower　A look down at the exhibition space from the second floor.

P.12・13	展示スペース床のステンレスライン
P.14	レセプションカウンター背面のタワーディテール
P.15 上	レセプションカウンター
P.15 左下	背面のタワーのディテール
P.15 右下	車体の色をサンプリングできるコーナー
P.12・13	The stainless steel on the floor.
P.14	The back of reception counter.
P.15 upper	The reception counter.
P.15 lower left	The detail of the back of reception counter.
P.15 lower right	Car body color sampling corner.

P.16・17	コーポレートコミュニケーションゾーン。イベントや展示が行われる
P.18	ブティックの外壁
P.19 上	ブティック入り口
P.19 中左	ブティックのレジカウンターを見る
P.19 中央	ブティック内を見る
P.19 中右	インターネットコーナー
P.16・17	The corporate communication zone.
P.18	The outside wall of the boutique.
P.19 upper	The entrance of the boutique.
P.19 middle left	The checkout counter in the boutique.
P.19 middle center	The boutique.
P.19 middle right	The Internet corner.

P.20・21　カフェ全景
P.21 上　カフェに通じるラウンジスペース
P.21 下　カフェのレジカウンター
P.20・21　The cafe.
P.21 upper　The lounge.
P.21 lower　The checkout counter of the cafe.

P.22　外壁のディテール
P.23 上　ファサード
P.23 左　ファサード見上げ
P.23 右　エントランス
P.22　　　The outside wall on the entrance.
P.23 upper　The facade.
P.23 left　　A look up at the entrance gate.
P.23 right　 The entrance.

Showroom
NISSAN GALLERY GINZA
Ginza, Tokyo
日産銀座ギャラリー
Completion : June 2001
Total area : 292㎡／
1F・197㎡　2F・95㎡

P.24 上　　　搬出入口
P.24 下　　　1階展示スペース
P.24・25　　展示スペースから2階フロアとレセプションを見る
P.24 upper　The delivery entrance.
P.24 lower　The display space.
P.24・25　　The reception from the display space.

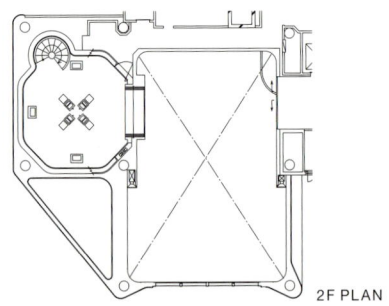

2F PLAN

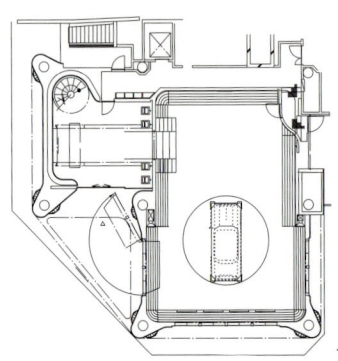

1F PLAN

P.26 上　　　搬出入口扉のヒンジ
P.26 左下、右下　同、ディテール
P.26　　　　　The detail of big door at the delivery entrance.

P.27 上　　　　　　　1階展示スペース床
P.27 左下、右下　　　1階展示スペースのコーナー部分
P.27 upper　　　　　 The detail of floor at the display space.
P.27 lower left・right The corner part in the display space.

P.28・29 2階から1階展示スペースを見下ろす
P.28・29 A look down at the display space from the second floor.

Among visually recognizable things, light is the most indefinite element. Of course, objectively speaking, light could be subjected to digital recognition, but it is not something we can actually feel. However, based on delusional ideas that turn these facts on their head - "what if light could be touched?" and "what if light could be made solid?" - I think of light as a design material, using such ideas as "soft light" and "rough light."

光は視覚認識できるものの中で、最も不確定な要素と考えています。もちろん、客観的に数値化認識は可能ですが、私たちはそれを実感できない。
それを逆手に取り、「光を触感できるとしたら」「光を固めることができたら」など妄想的な仮説に基づいて、
「柔らかい光」「ざらざらした光」というように「光を素材化する」ことを考えています。

P.30　1階階段室の壁面
P.31　2階への螺旋階段
P.30　The wall in the staircase.
P.31　The spiral staircase to the second floor.

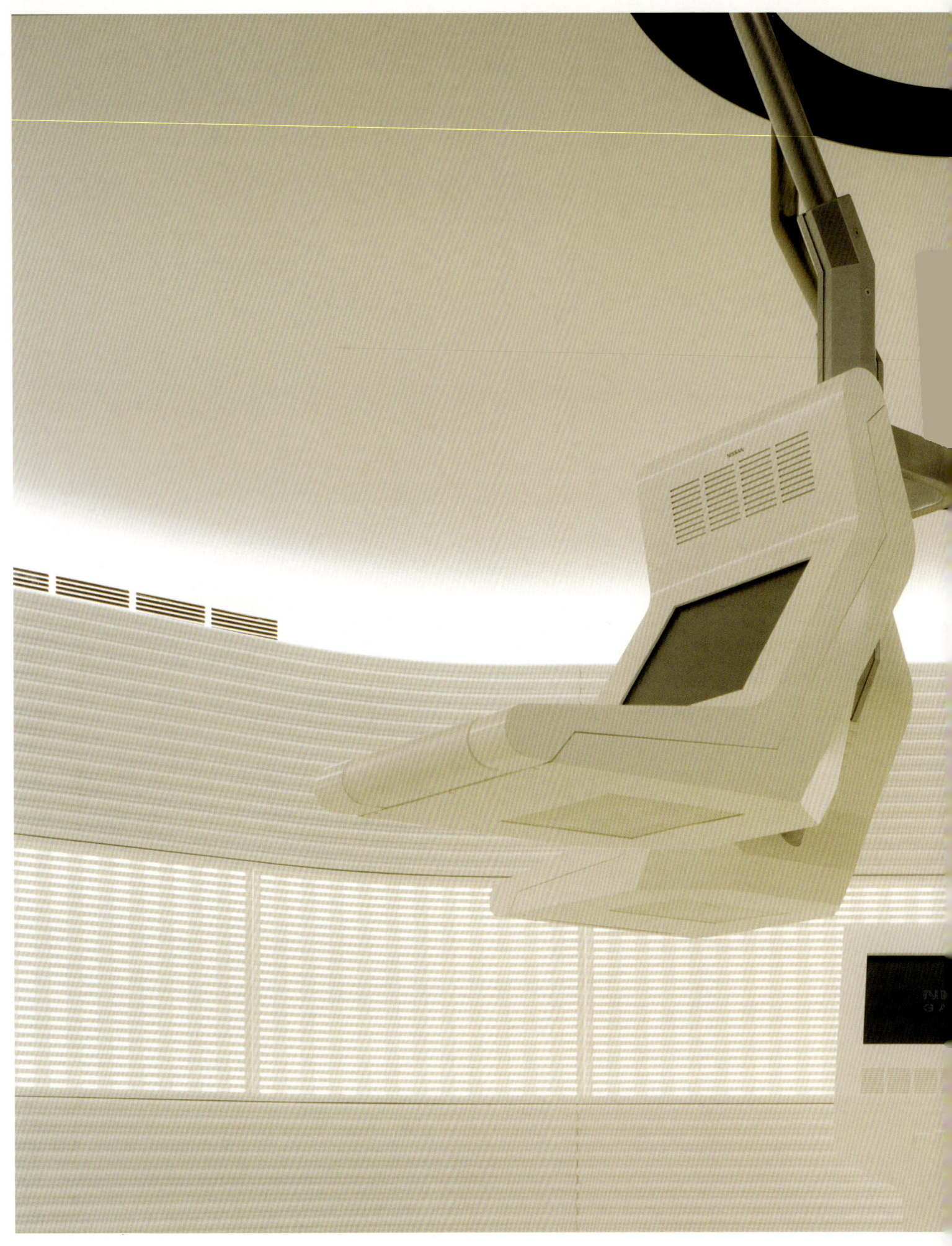

P.32・33　2階「デジタルギャラリー」
P.34・35　外壁
P.32・33　The digital gallery on the second floor.
P.34・35　The outside wall.

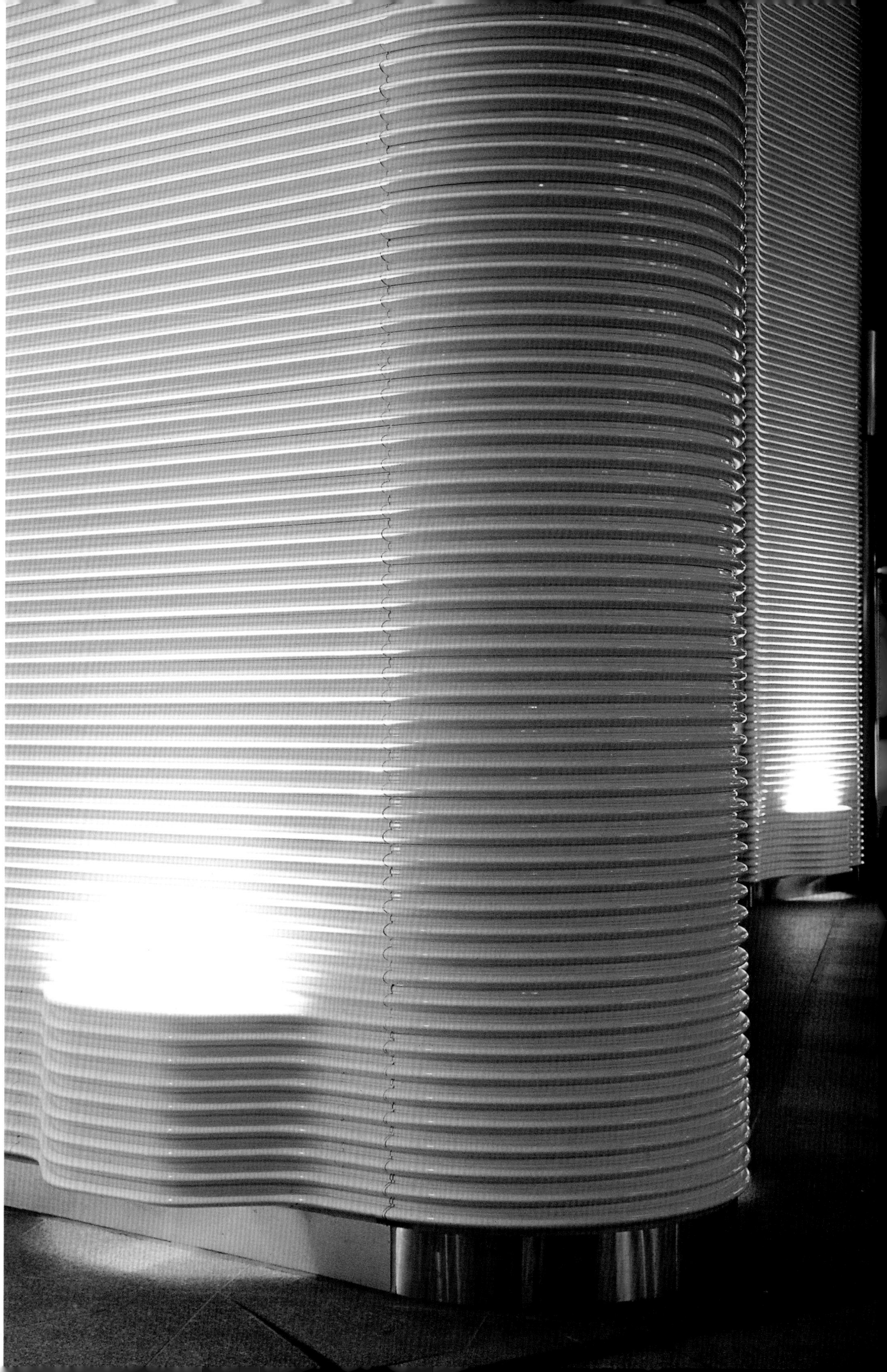

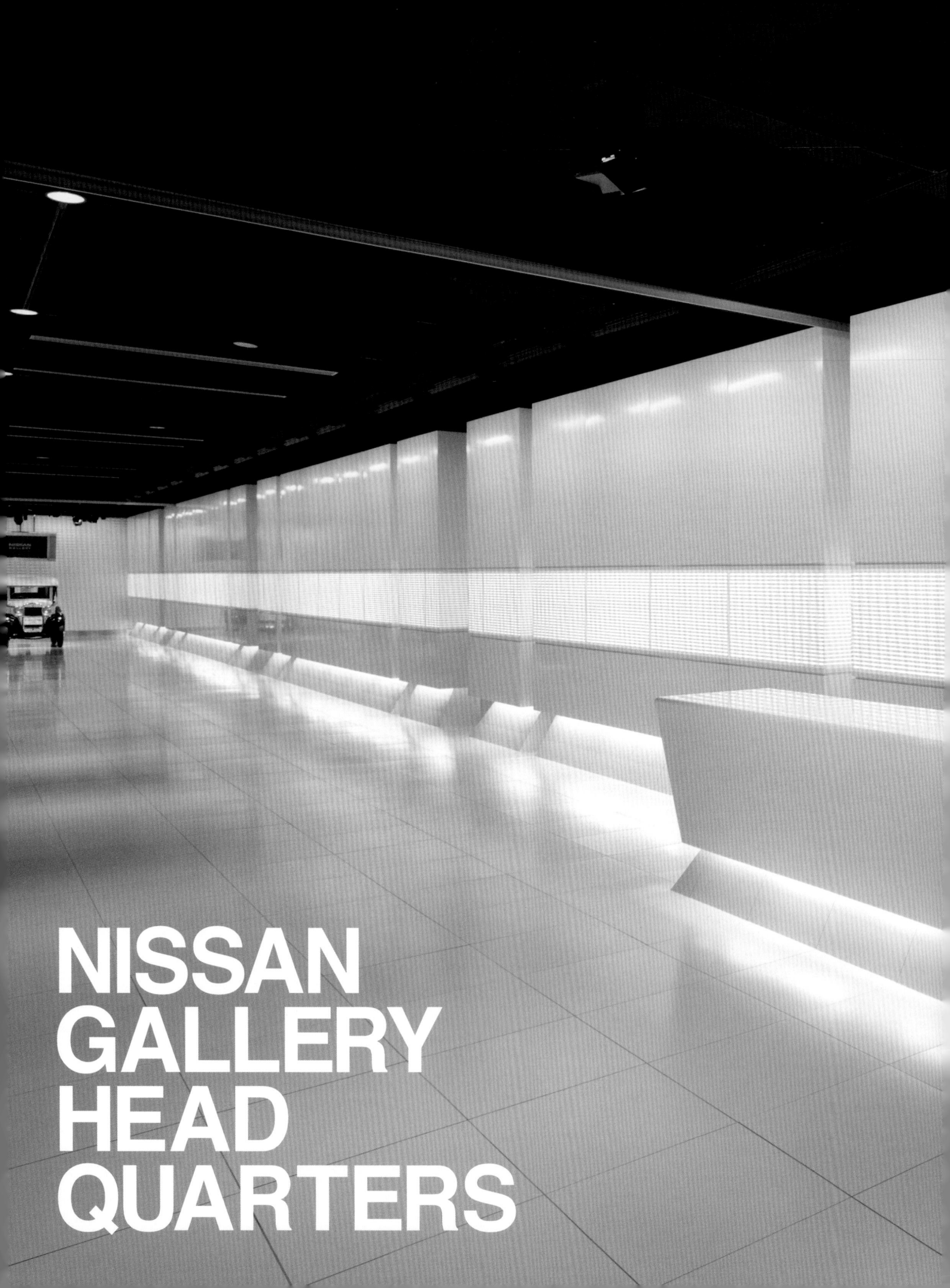

NISSAN GALLERY HEAD QUARTERS

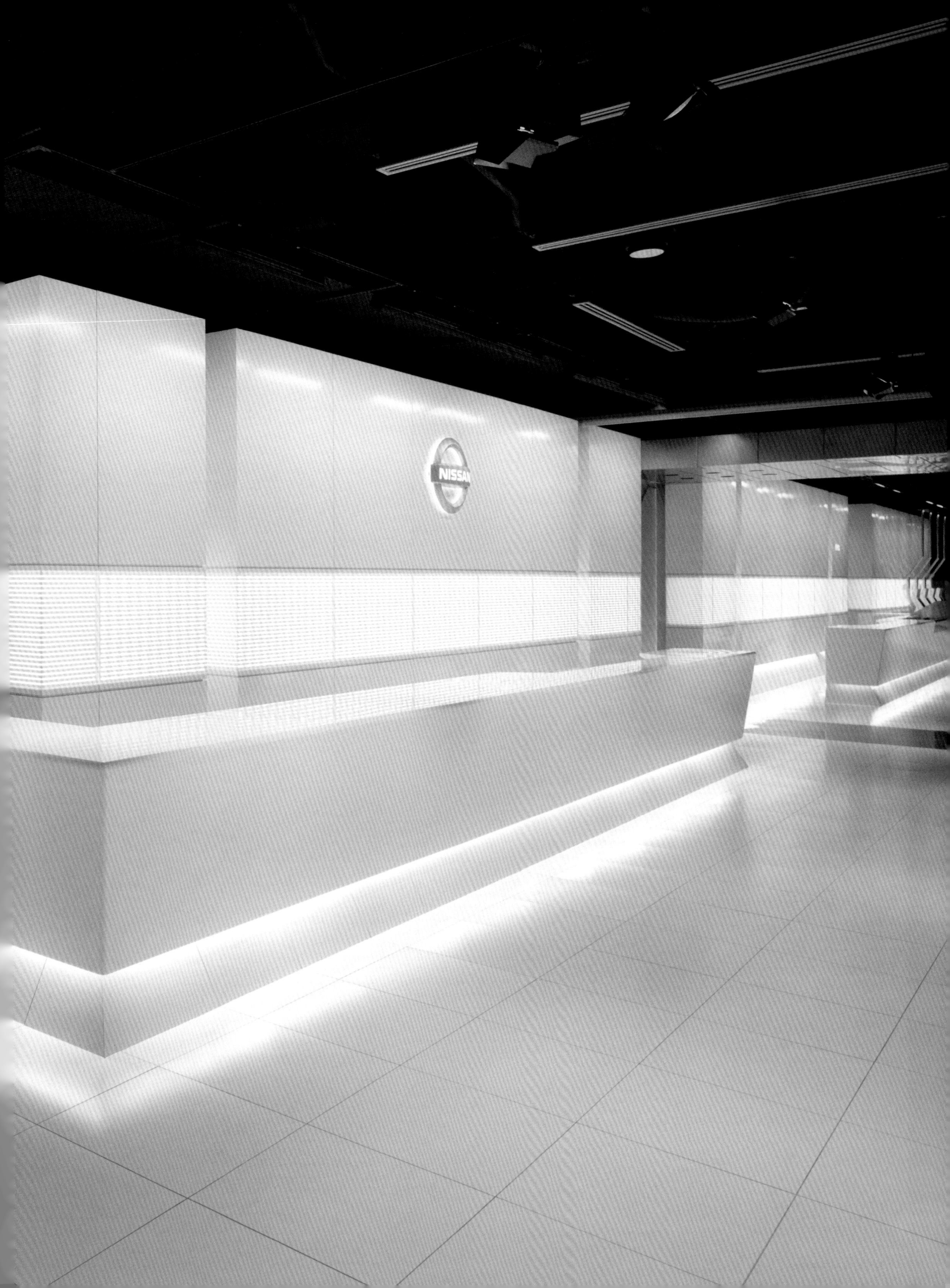
NISSAN

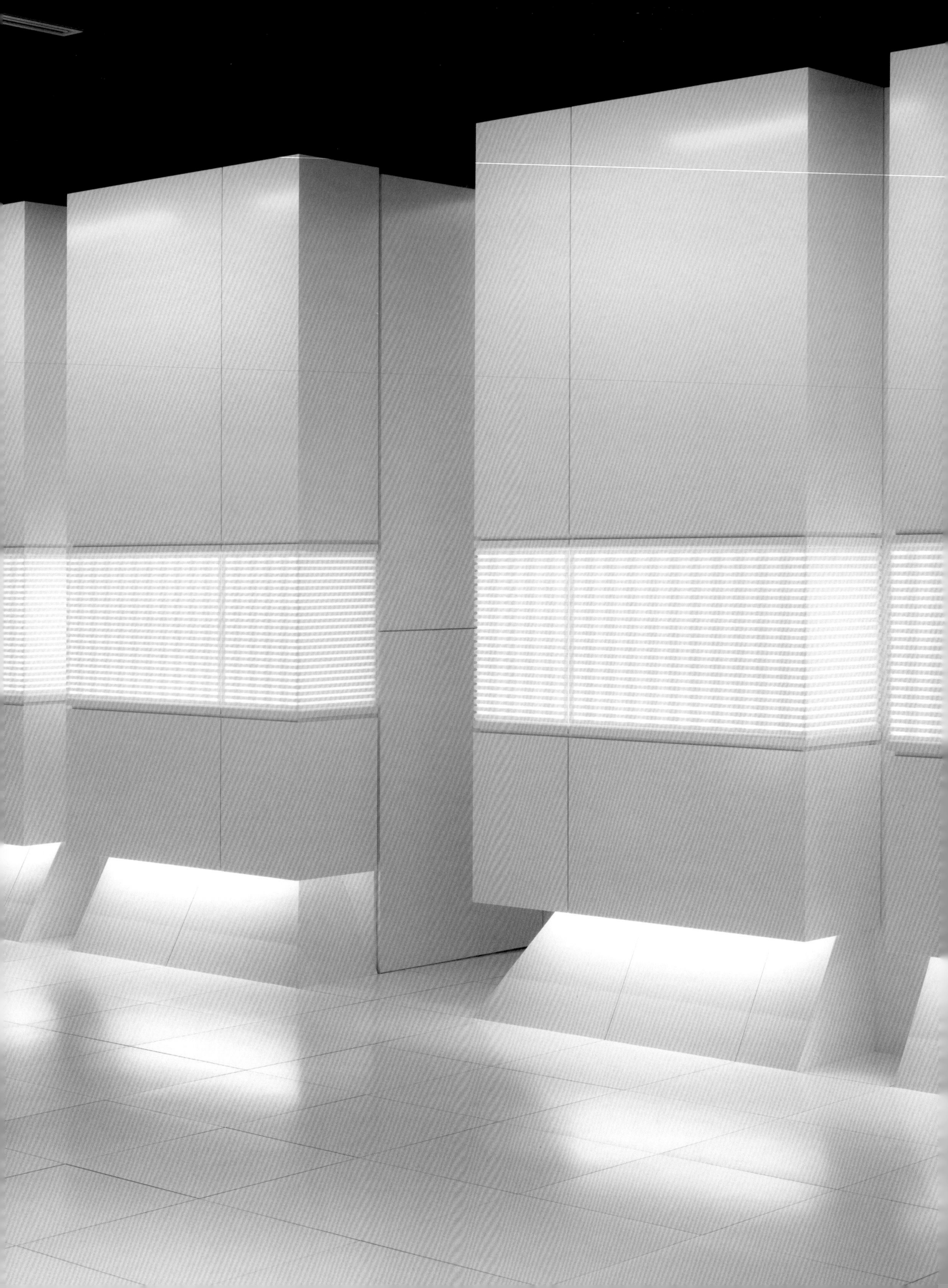

Showroom
NISSAN GALLERY HEADQUARTERS (old)
Ginza, Tokyo
日産本社ギャラリー（旧本社）
Completion : June 2001　Total area : 1111㎡

P.36・37　インフォメーションカウンターを見る
P.38　　　ギャラリーの光り壁
P.39　　　モニターで製品の情報を検索できるコーナー
P.36・37　The information counter.
P.38　　　The lighted wall of the display space.
P.39　　　The information corner.

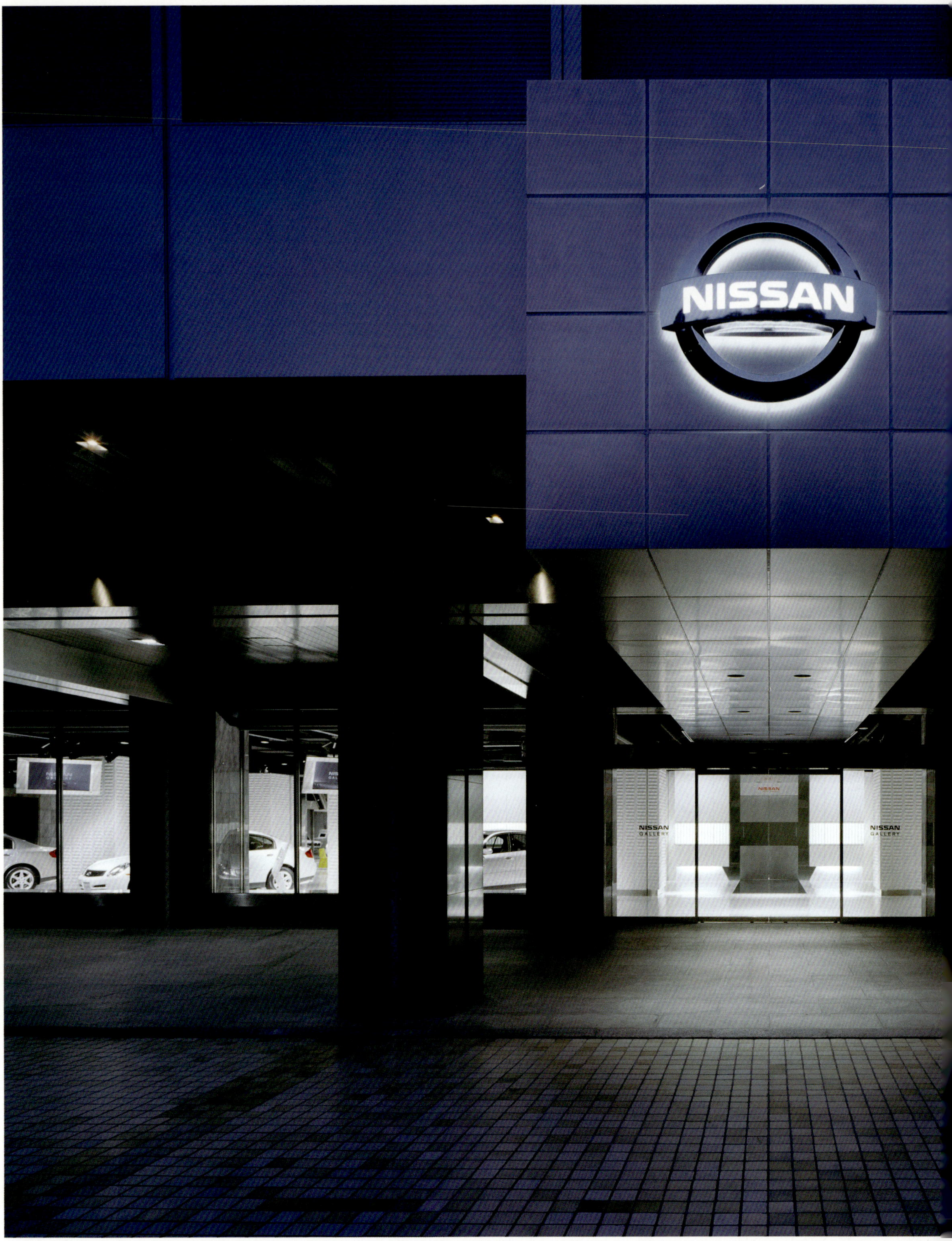
NISSAN

P.40・41	エントランスアプローチ
P.41 上	カフェのレジカウンター
P.41 下	男性用トイレ
P.40・41	The approach.
P.41 upper	The checkout counter on the cafe.
P.41 lower	The men's room.

NISSAN GALLERY SAPPORO

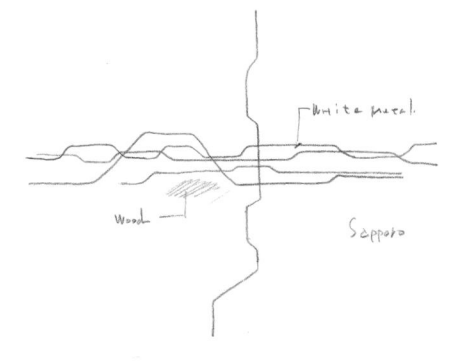

Showroom
NISSAN GALLERY SAPPORO
Sapporo, Hokkaido
日産札幌ギャラリー
Completion : October 2004
Total area : 699㎡ / 1F・276㎡ 2F・423㎡

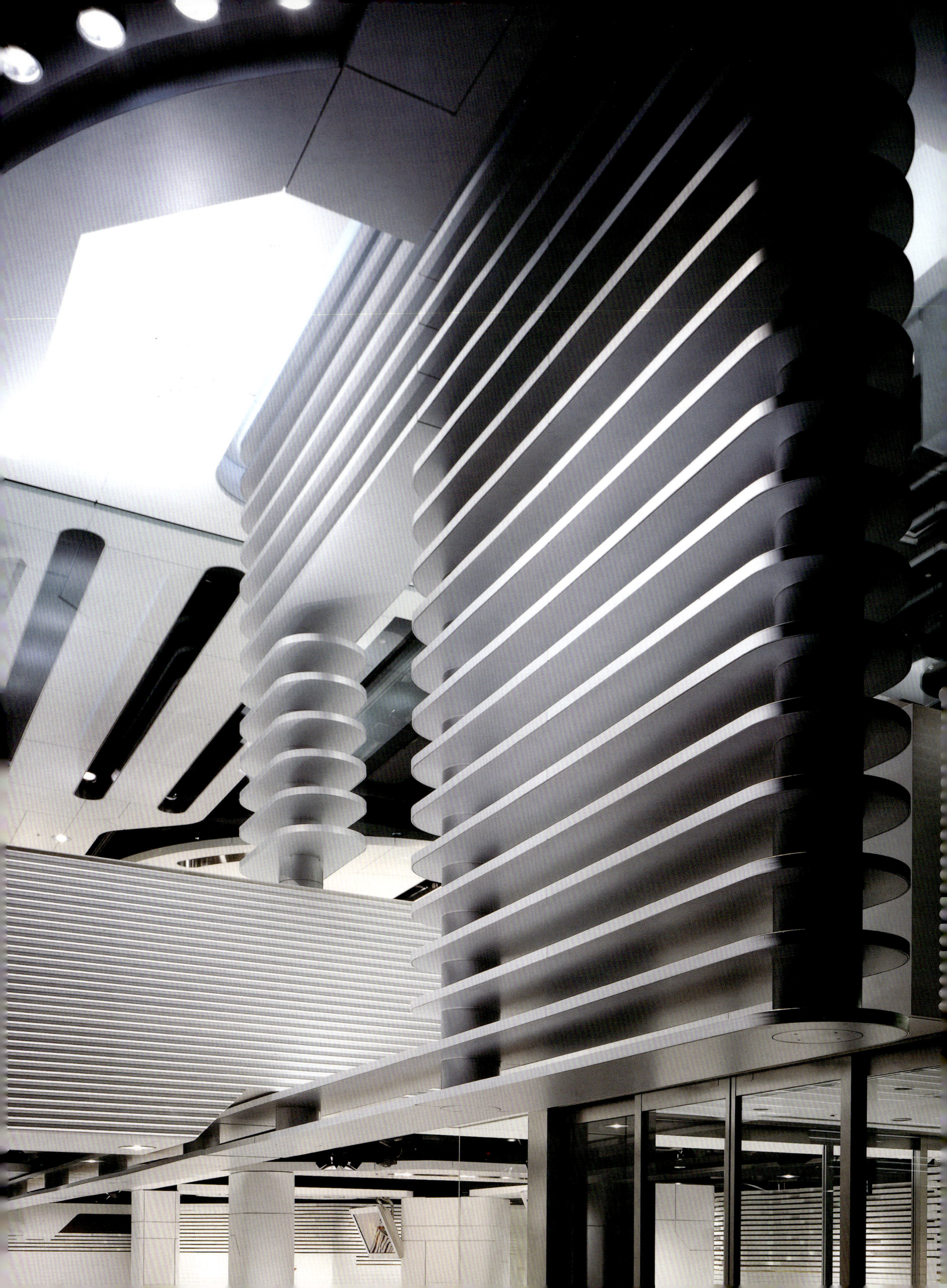

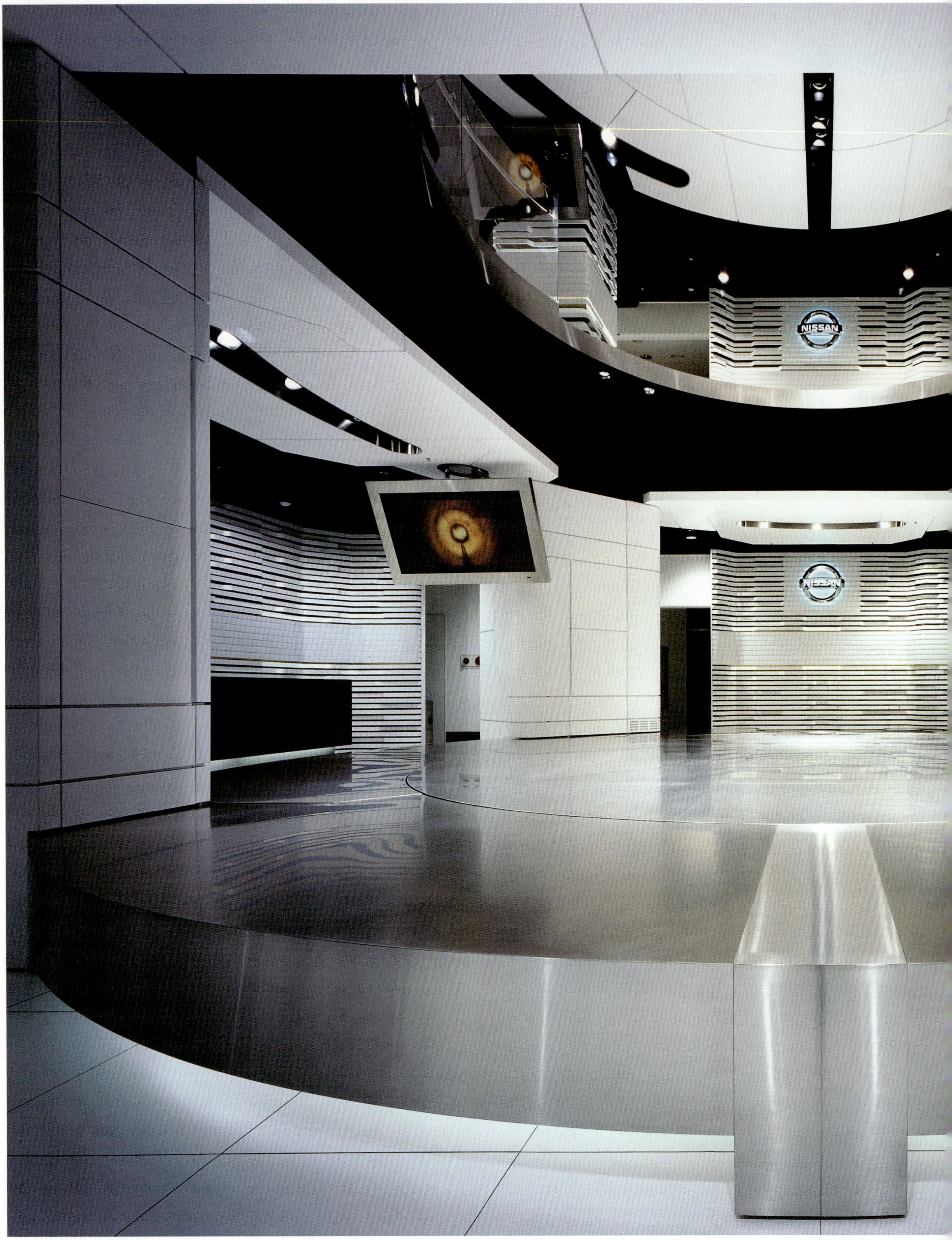
NISSAN
NISSAN

P.42	アルミルーバーで仕切られたギャラリー奥の通路
P.43	外観の一部を見上げる
P.44・45	展示スペース。中央にはターンテーブルがある
P.45右	車を載せ上昇するターンテーブル
P.46・47	外観
P.42	The inside of the passage.
P.43	A look up at the outside wall.
P.44・45	The display space.
P.45 right	The turntable that puts car and rises of the display space.
P.46・47	The facade.

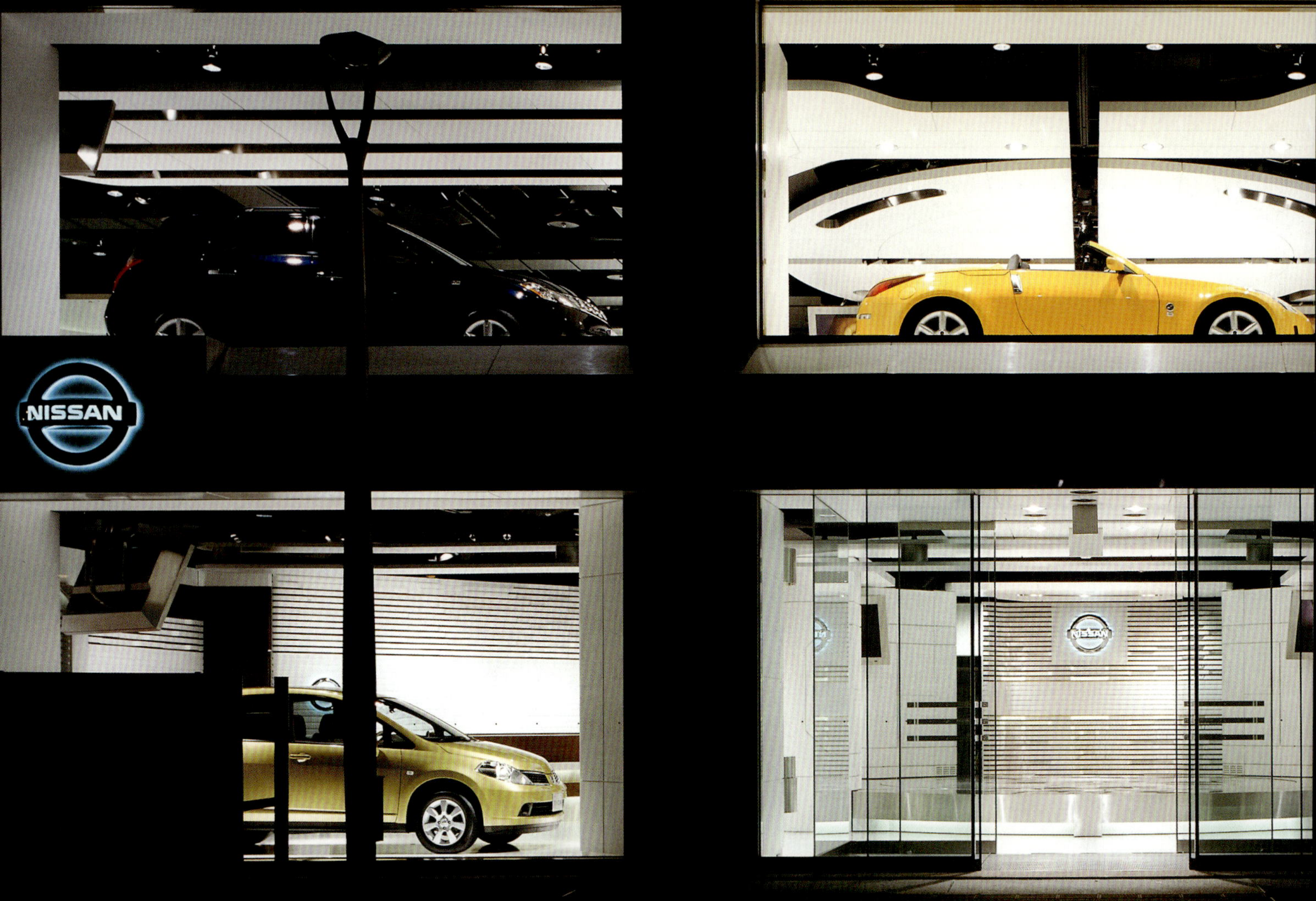
NISSAN

NISSAN
GALLERY
SAPPORO

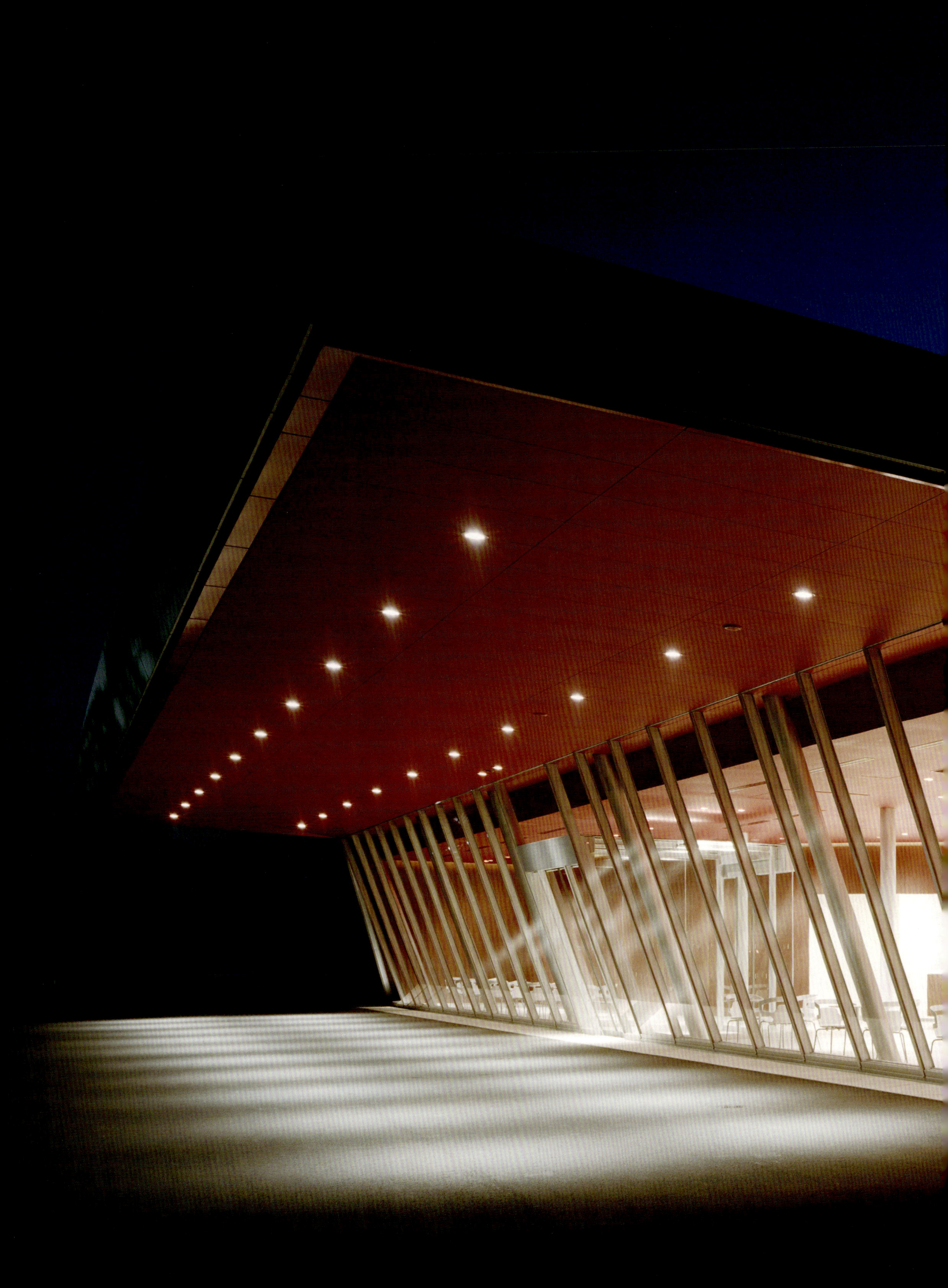

NISSAN GRANDRIVE

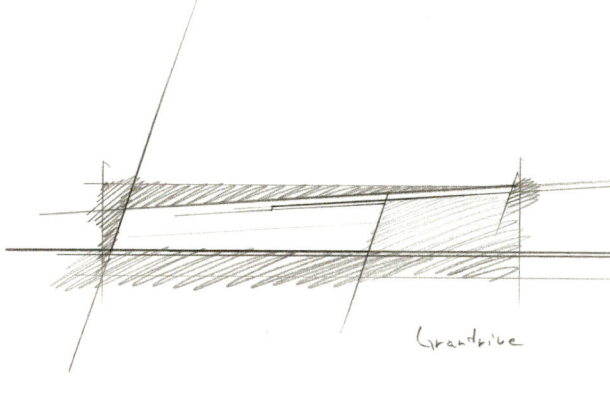

Guest Hall
NISSAN GRANDRIVE
Yokosuka, Kanagawa
日産グランドライブ
Completion : September 2007
Total area : 741㎡

P.48・49	外観
P.50 上下	外観
P.51 上・中左	車寄せ
P.51 中右	施設ゲートのロゴ
P.51 下	レセプションホールを見る
P.48・49	The exterior.
P.50 upper・lower	The exterior.
P.51 upper & left	The porch.
P.51 lower right	The logotype on the gate.
P.51 lower	A view of the reception hall from the outside.

When I was trying to get from an old method, the "Japanese expression a were a good hint.
I had found words to exp
Even if it cannot be seen the feeling behind the ex "at the DNA level" definit in my special expressio and I interpret it to be so I will eventually be able

away
words
t the DNA level"

ress what I felt.
 with the eyes,
pression
ely is used
n,
mething
to read.

手垢のついた方法から脱すべきだと考え、
模索していた私にとって、「DNAレベルでの日本の表現」という言葉は
とても良いヒントになりました。
感覚を表す言葉が見つかった、という感じです。
そのDNAレベルでの表現という感覚は、
視覚的に表出はしていなくとも、空間表現に確実に作用して、
読み取ることができる存在になるものと解釈しています。

THE 35TH TOKYO MOTOR SHOW NISSAN BOOTH

Motorshow Booth
THE 35TH TOKYO MOTOR SHOW
NISSAN BOOTH
Makuhari, Chiba
第35回東京モーターショー 日産ブース
Completion : October 2001
Total area : 3035㎡

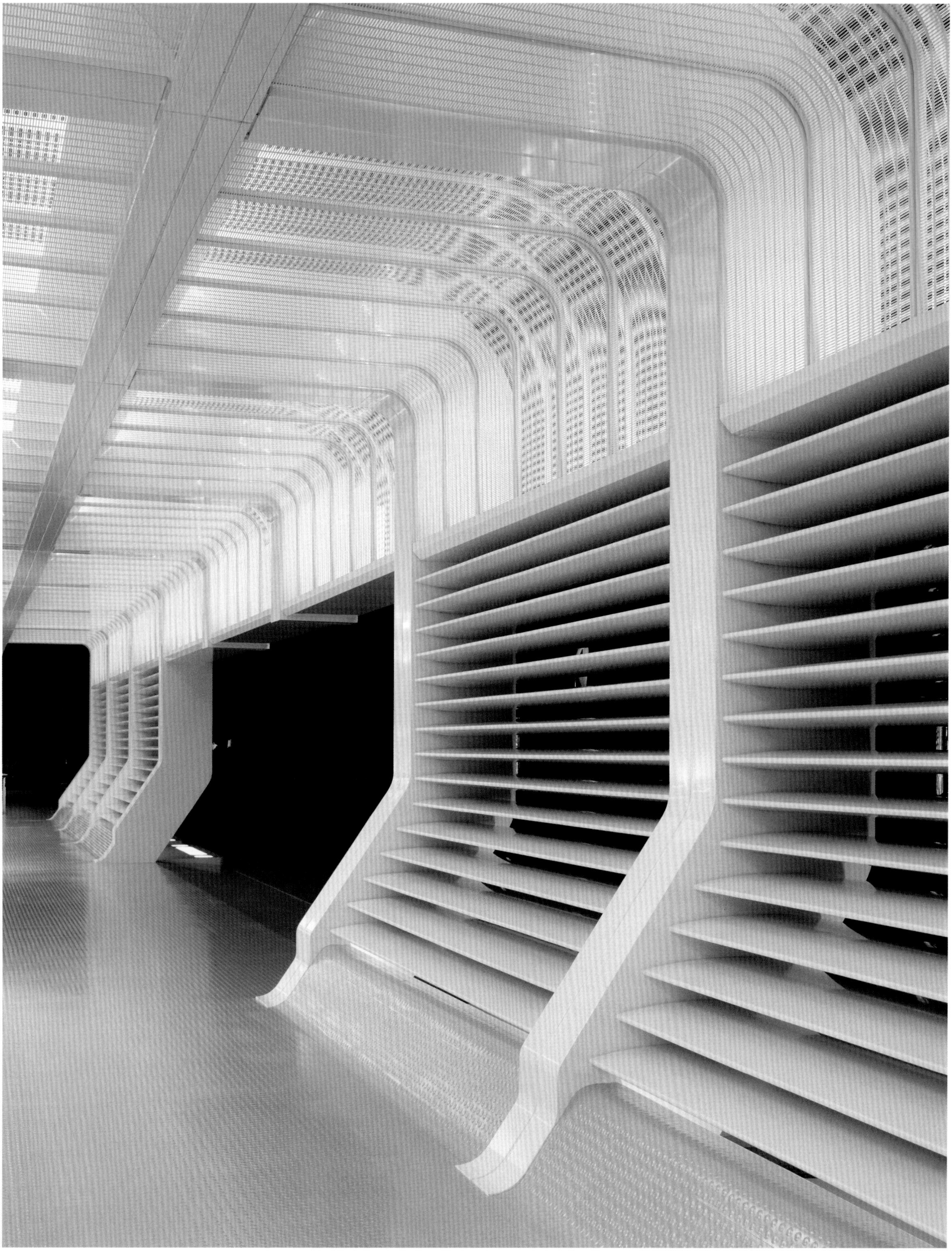

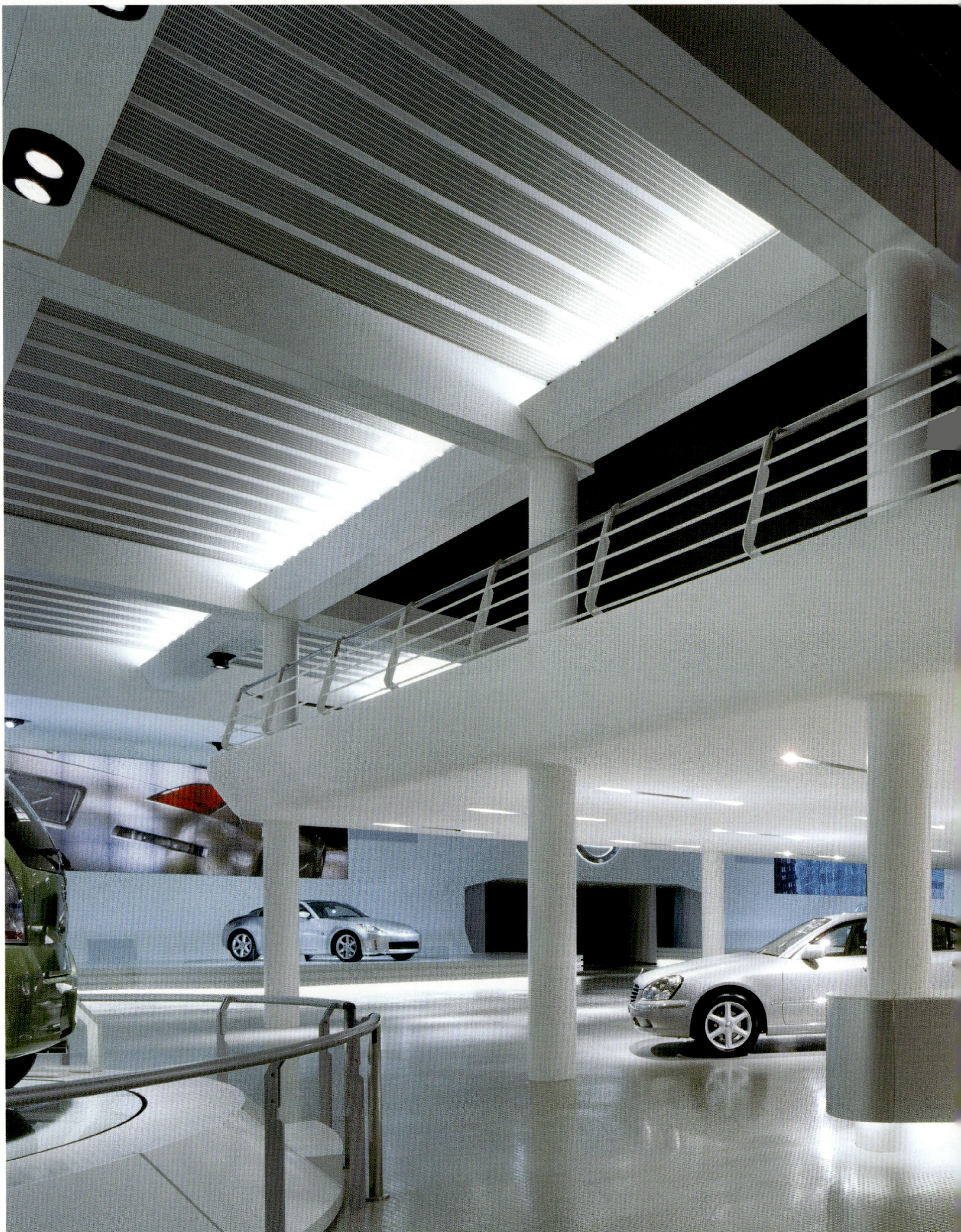

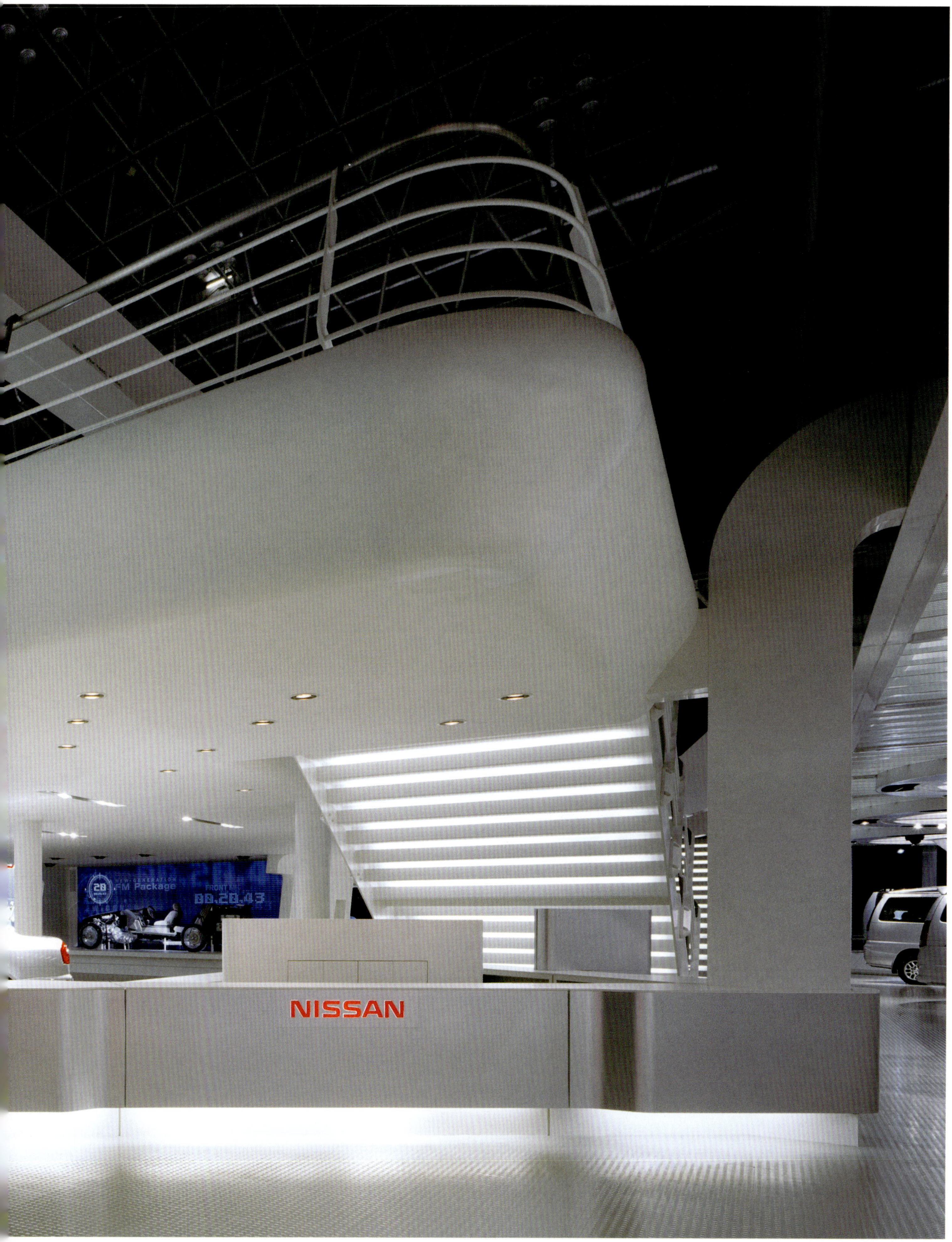
FM Package
NISSAN

P.54	ブース内のインフォメーションモニター
P.55	ルーバー壁面
P.56・57	展示スペース
P.58・59	同
P.59 上	ブースを見下ろす
P.59 下	2階展示スペースへの階段
P.54	The information display.
P.55	The louver wall.
P.56・57	The exhibition space.
P.58・59	Ditto.
P.59 upper	A look down at the booth.
P.59 lower	The staircase to the second floor.

59

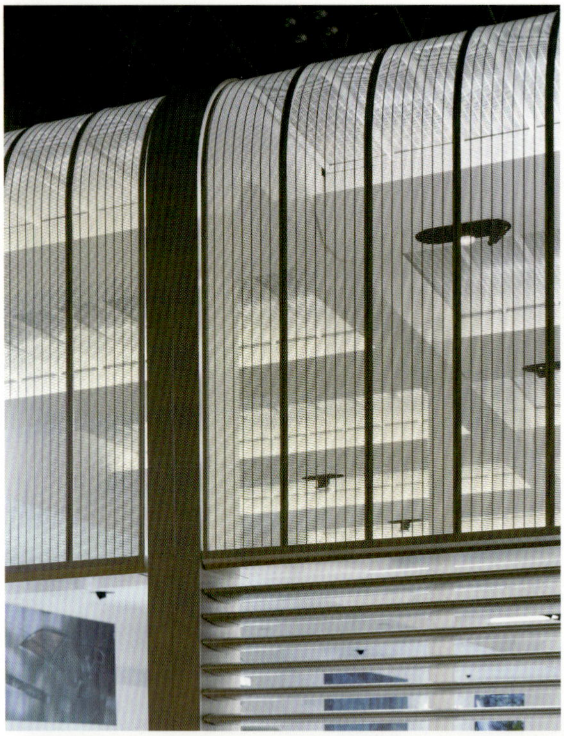

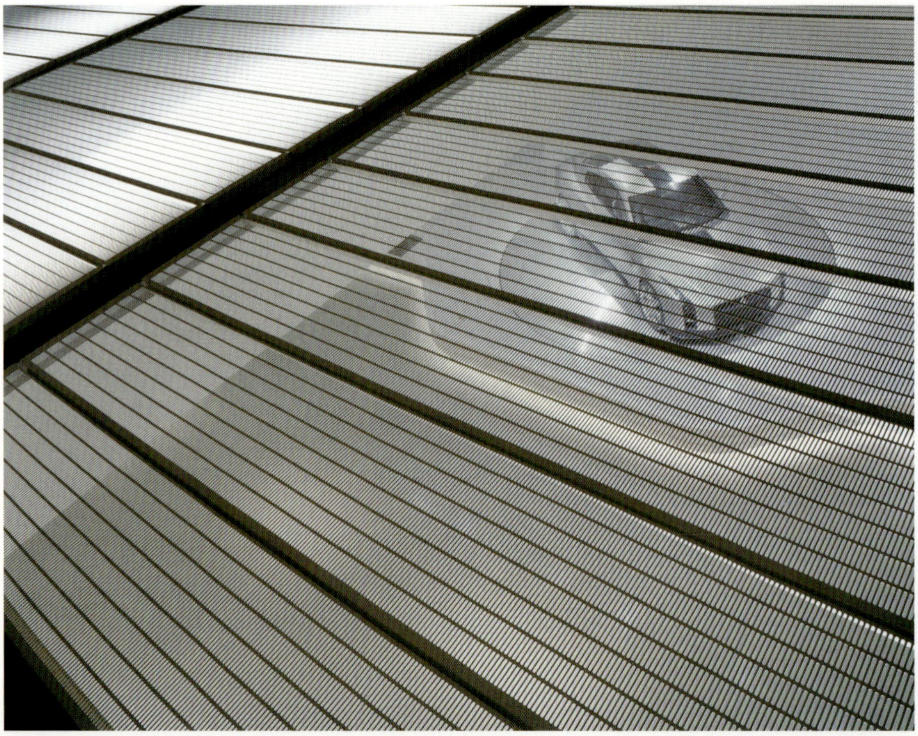

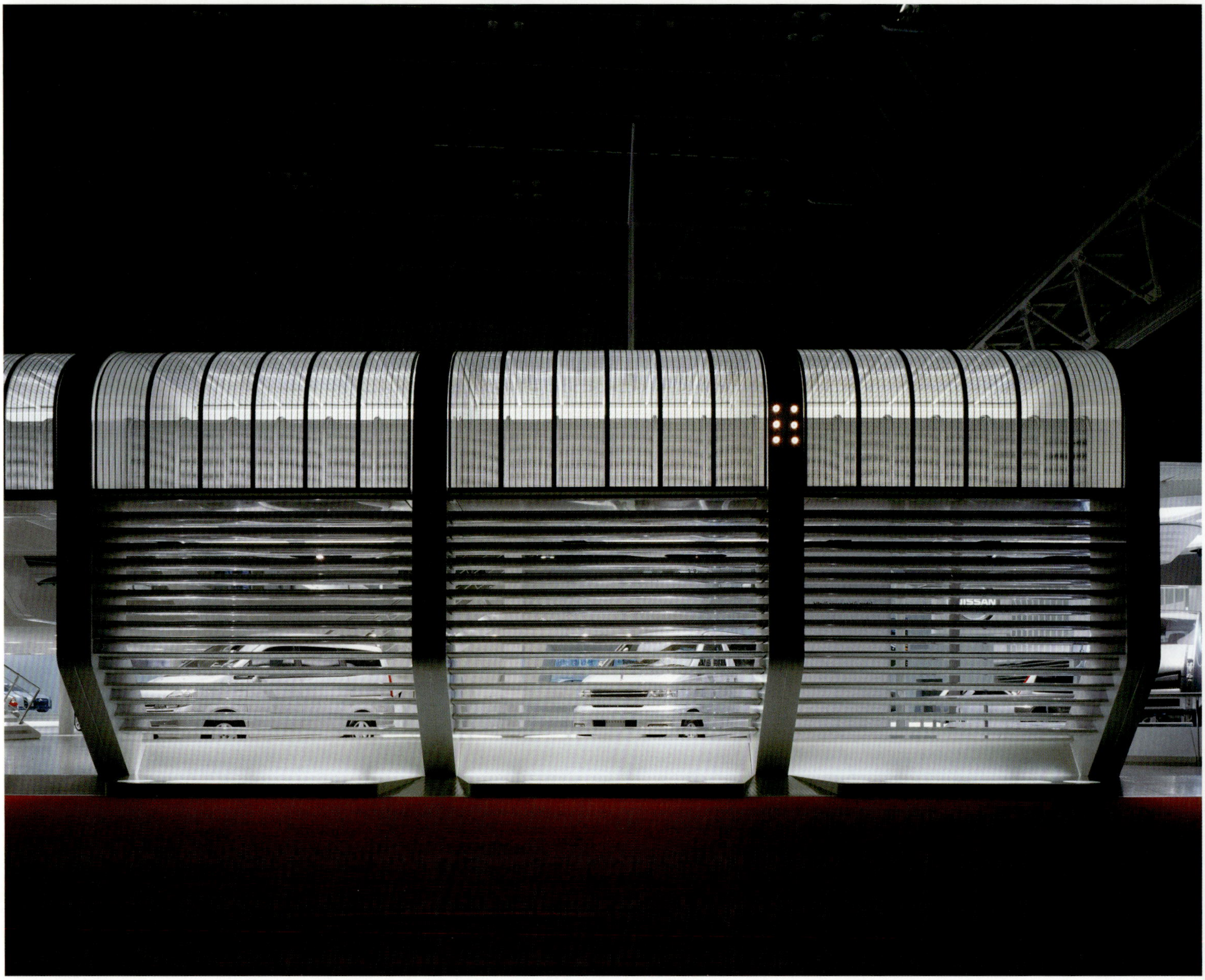

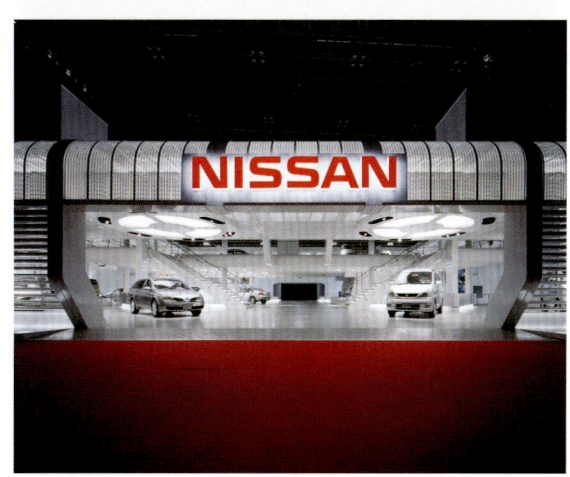

P.60 上下	外部から見たブース壁面、屋根
P.61 上	外部から展示スペースを見る
P.61 左右	メーンエントランス
P.60 upper & lower	The wall & the ceiling of the booth.
P.61 upper	A view of the exhibition space from the outside.
P.61 left & right	The main entrance.

THE 36TH TOKYO MOTOR SHOW NISSAN BOOTH

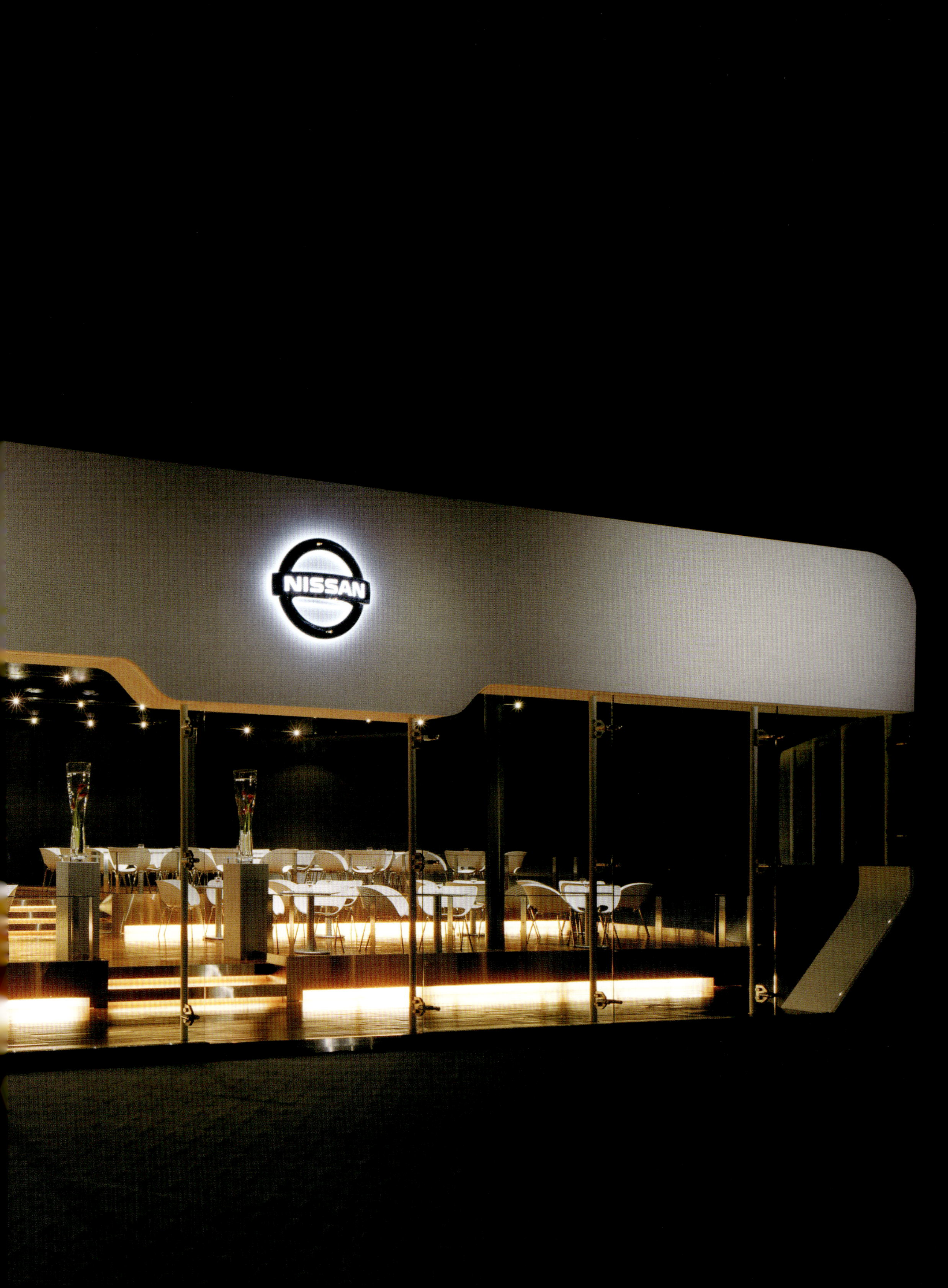
NISSAN

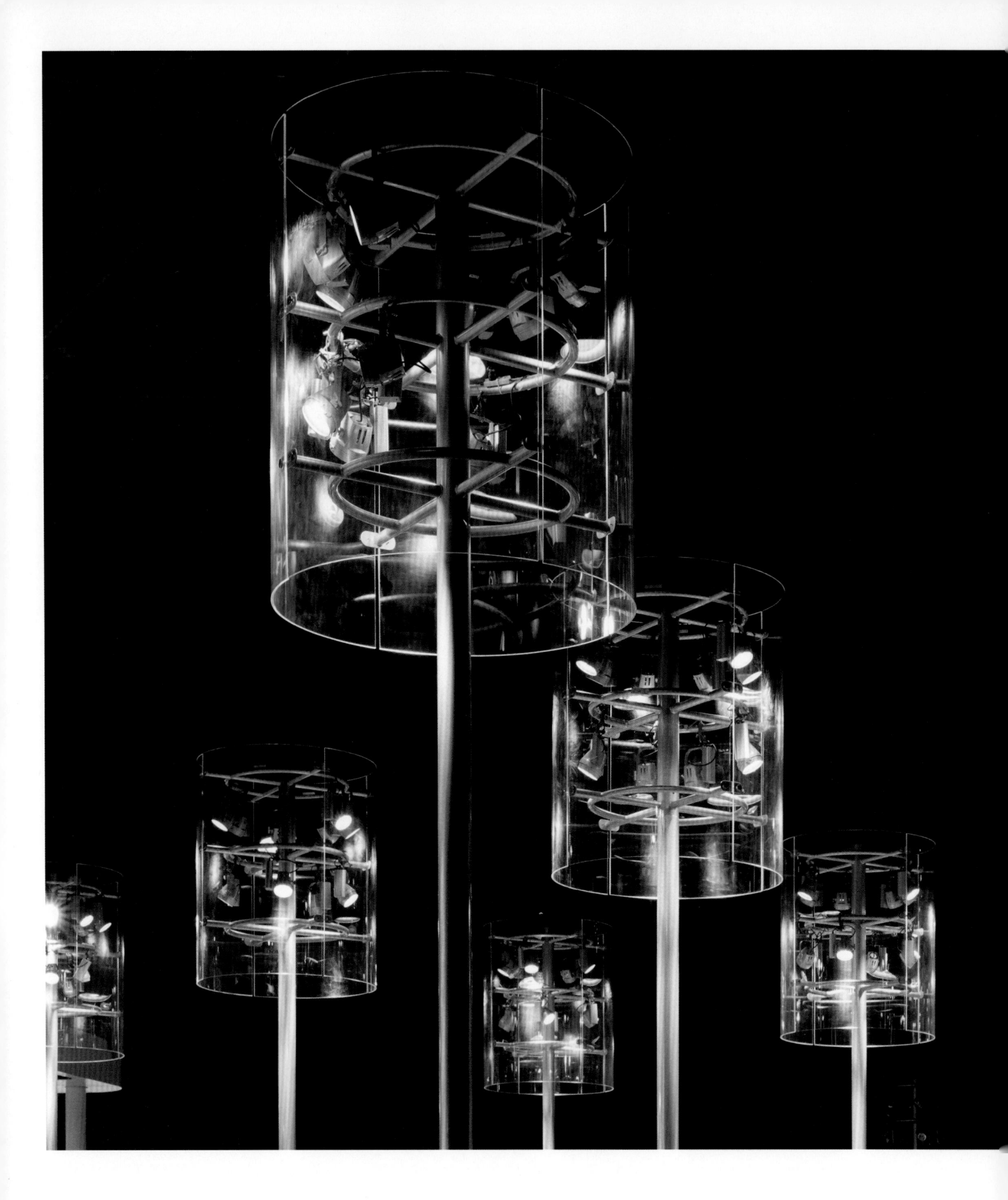

Motorshow Booth
THE 36TH TOKYO MOTOR SHOW
NISSAN BOOTH
Makuhari, Chiba
第36回東京モーターショー　日産ブース
Completion : October 2002
Total area : 2000㎡

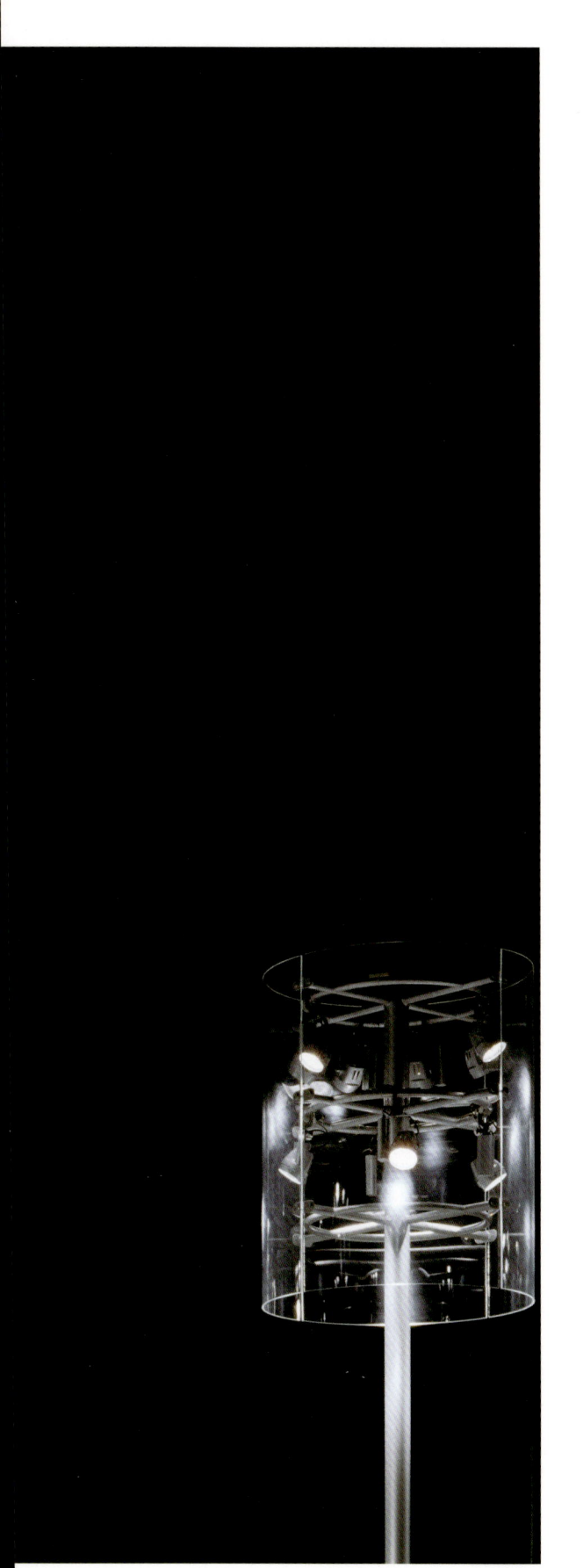

P.62・63	ブース内の商談スペース
P.64・65	オリジナルの照明ポール
P.65 上	メーンエントランス
P.65 下	商談スペース
P.62・63	The business meeting space.
P.64・65	The lighting pole.
P.65 upper	The main entrance.
P.65 lower	The business meeting space.

THE 37TH TOKYO MOTOR SHOW NISSAN BOOTH

P.66・67 上	ブースを見下ろす
P.66・67 下	展示スペースはラウンドするスクリーンにより空間全体の色が変わる
P.68・69	ブース外観、展示スペース、ルーバー壁面など
P.66・67 upper	A look down at the booth.
P.66・67 lower	The exhibition space that changes color.
P.68・69	The exterior & the interior of the booth.

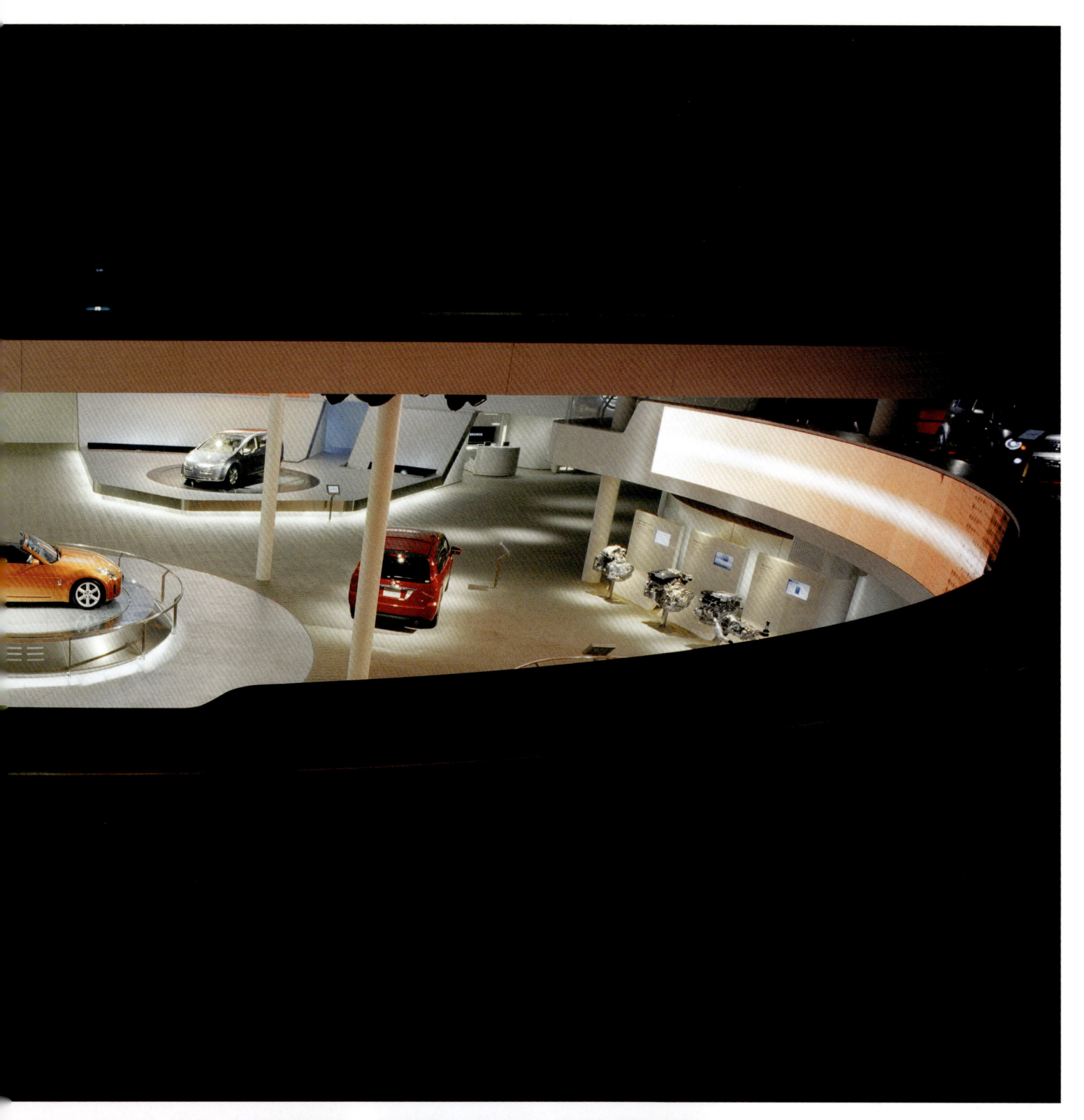

Motorshow Booth
THE 37TH TOKYO MOTOR SHOW NISSAN BOOTH
Makuhari, Chiba
第37回東京モーターショー　日産ブース
Completion : October 2003　Total area : 2757㎡

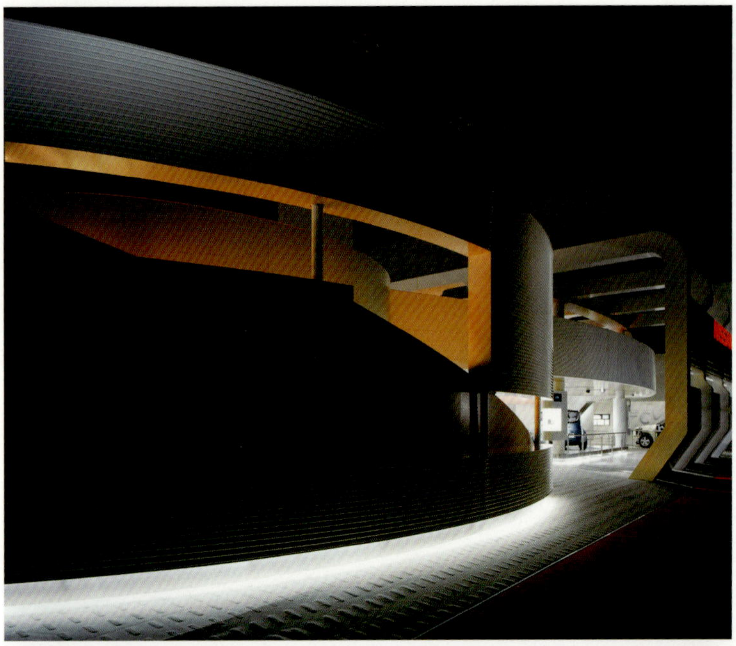
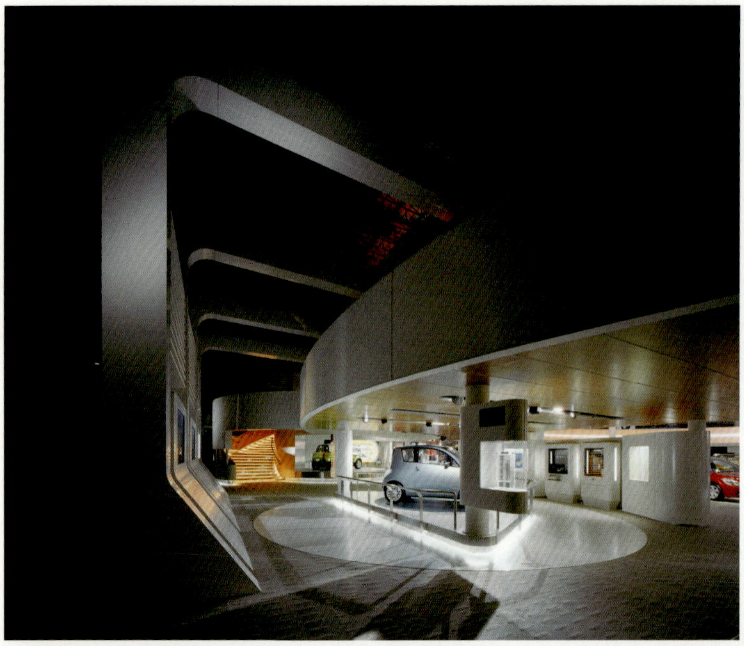
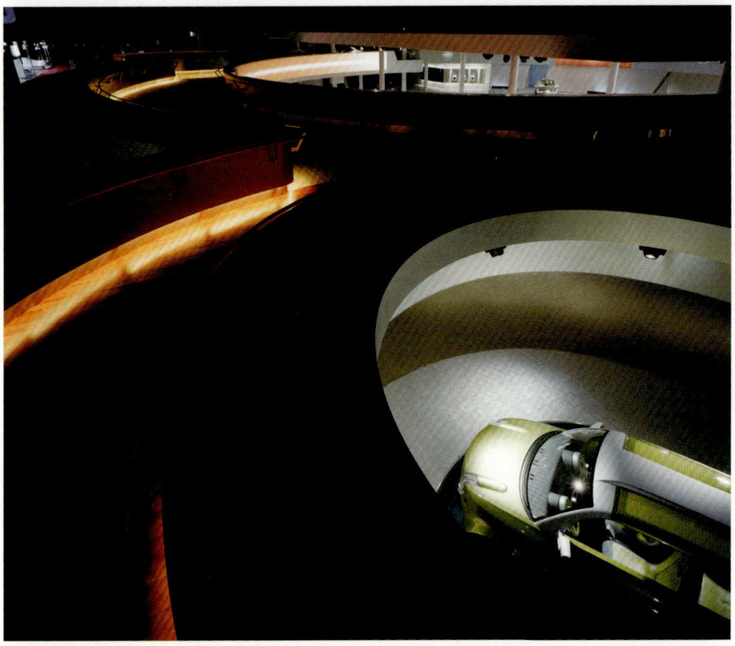
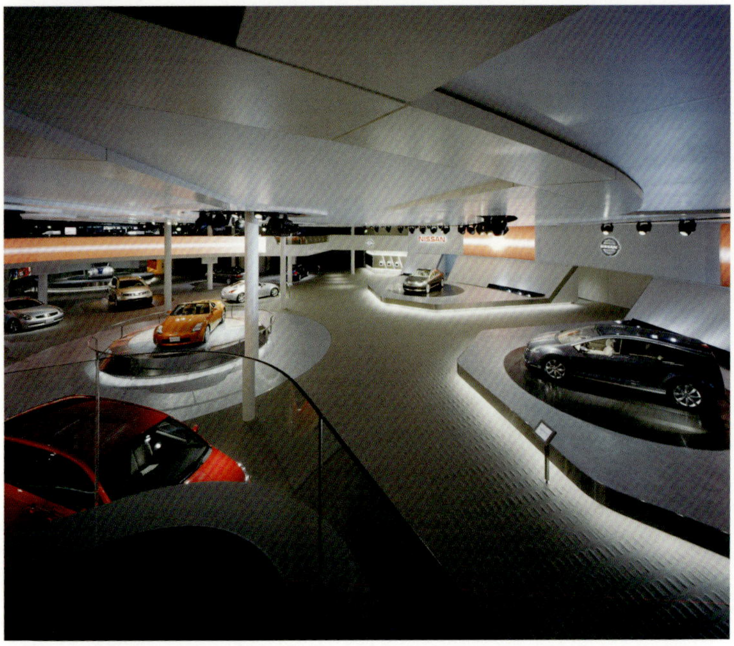
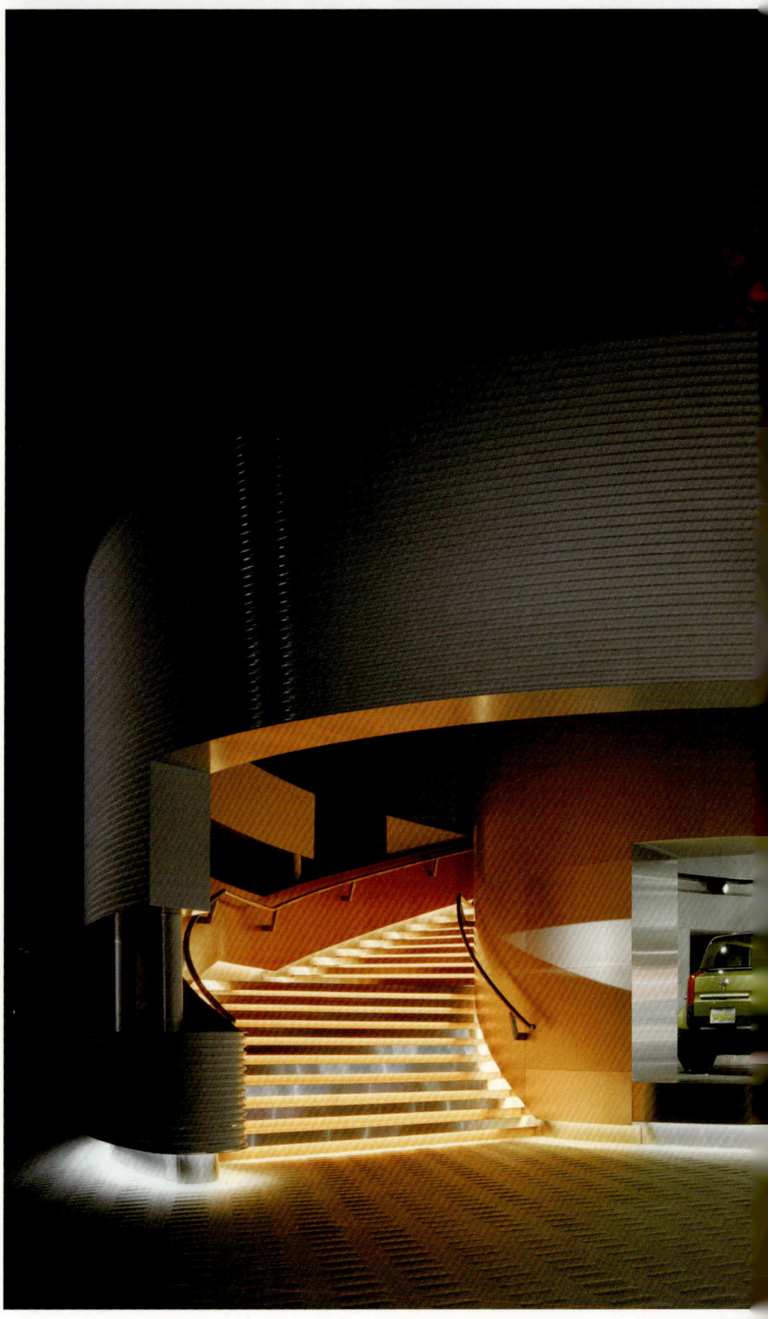

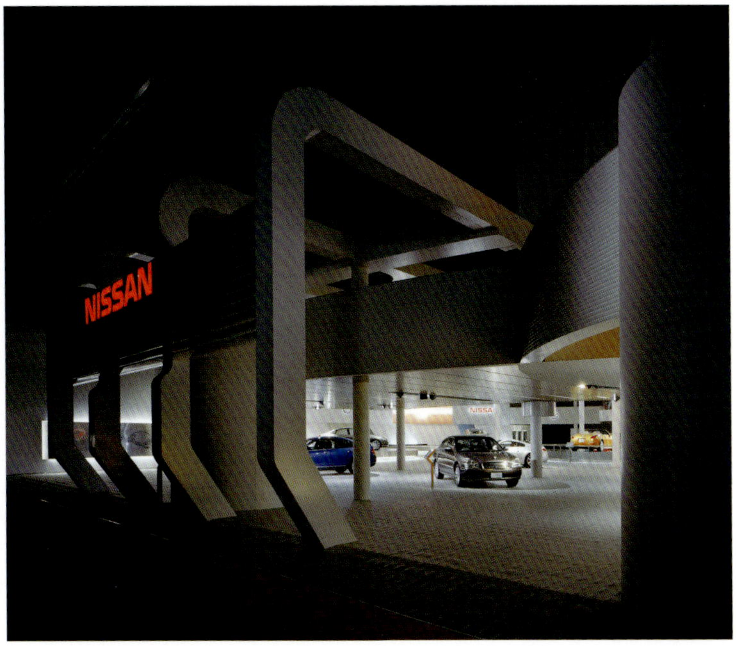
NISSAN

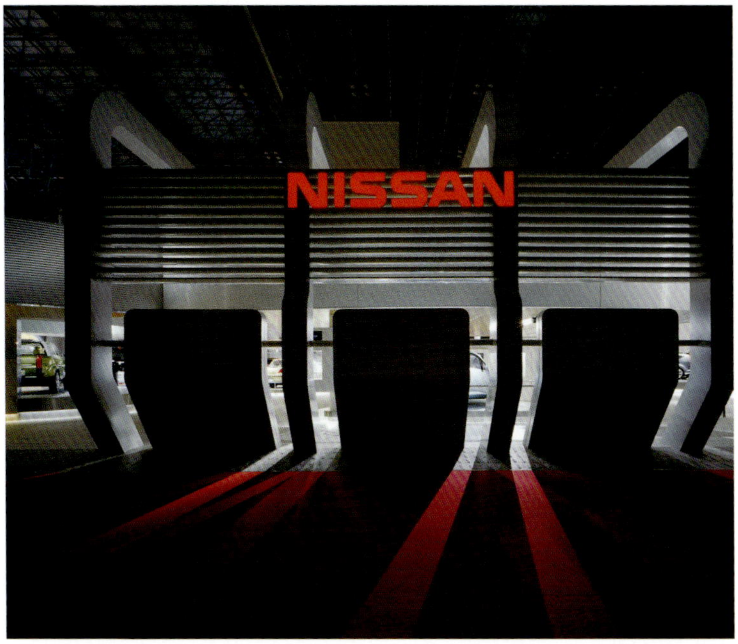
NISSAN

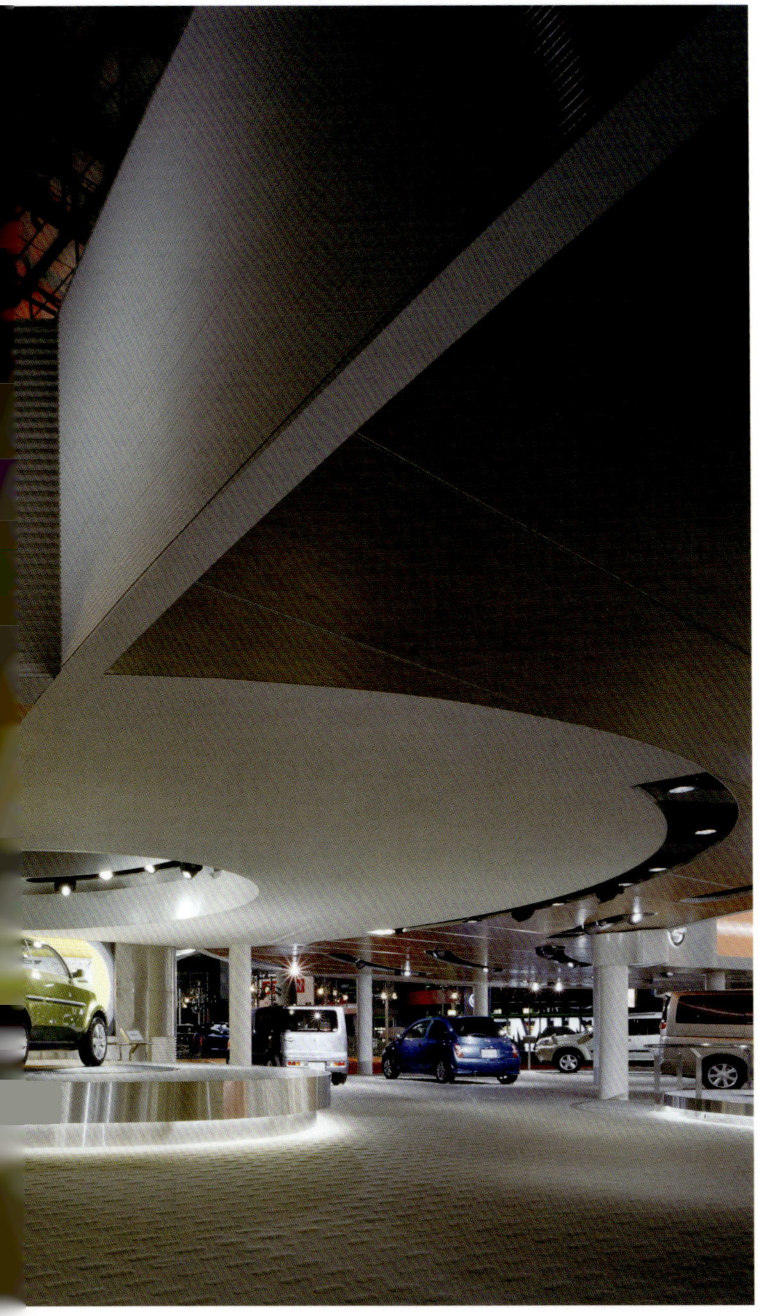

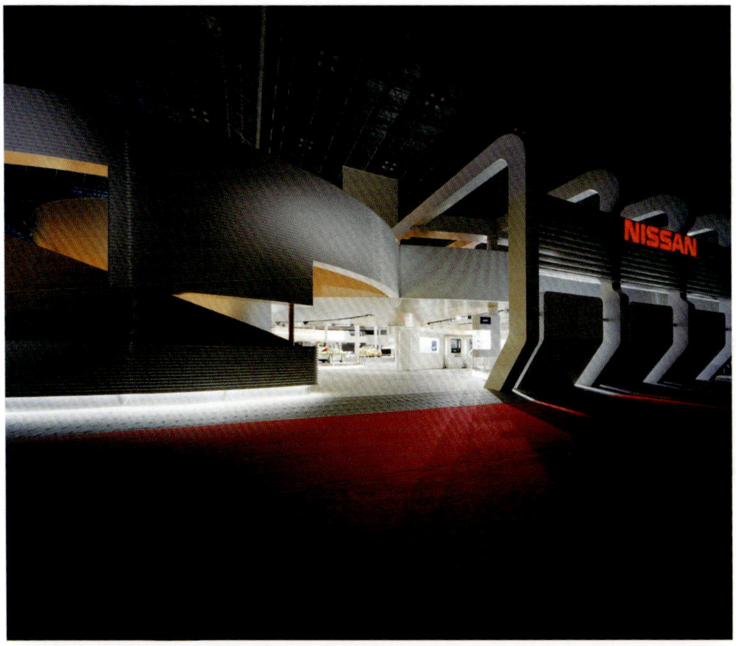
NISSAN

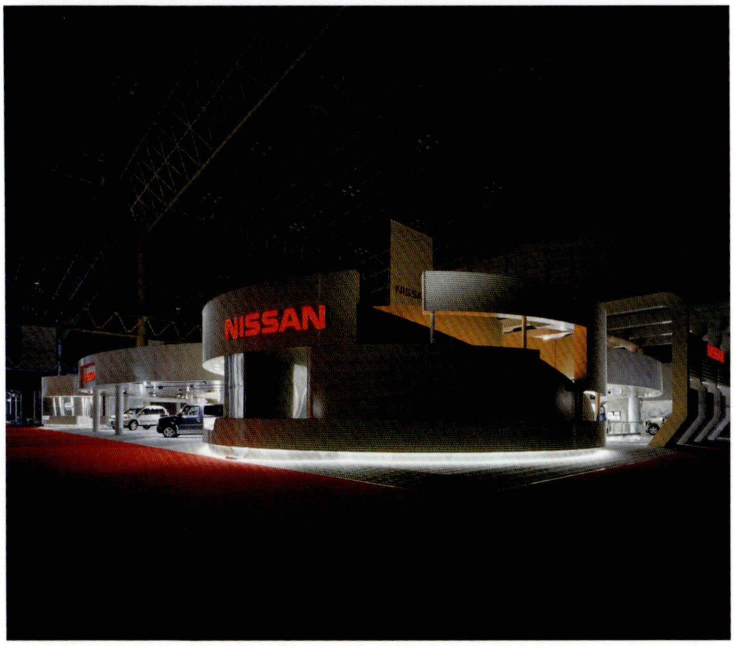
NISSAN

INTERVIEW 1

Q. 文田さんのアプローチはとても建築的だと思いますが、どういうデザイン・プロセスでしょうか。

文田 まず、空間を構築する際、例えば「床・壁・天井」という「言葉」に縛られない、ということがあります。例えば、ある一つの物事に関して、日常では、そのもの自体の名称を言葉にすることによって自身で理解するわけですが、これまでにない何か突き抜けたモノをつくりたいと思った時、日常、目にするものから疑ってみて、もの自体の「言葉」を外した時に何が見えてくるか、ということをよく考えます。

空間づくりにおいては、床・壁・天井が厳然たる要素として存在しますが、それを本来の意味から外すことで、どういう空間表現に落とし込めるのか。人は、一般的な四角い部屋を想像するとき、地面に対して垂直にあるものを「壁」、壁と垂直にあるものを「床」「天井」と認識していますが、言葉にすると平滑なイメージになってしまう。しかし実際には、床も壁も天井も、歪んでいたり曲面だったり、ねじれていたりすることがあります。例えば、それらが一つの面で繋がって球体のようになった場合、床・壁・天井を明確に切り取ることはできない。たとえ切り取ったとしても、人によって、また時代や文化によっても、その認識には大きな違いが出てくるはずです。

こういった考え方は、以前読んだ「虹」に関する記号論の話がヒントになっています。虹とは、目で見える光の色の最大幅ですが、その色をどこで分節するかという判断は、場所や時代によって異なります。子供の頃から"虹は七色"という文化に慣れ親しんできて、どこかで七つに切り取って考えなければいけないと思っていました。しかし本当は無段階で、人によって一つの色と色の間はとても曖昧で、例えば同じ七色でも分節する場所はそれぞれ異なります。

空間の構成要素も同じように、曖昧な言葉で認識しているようなものなので、そういった言葉がなければどういう風になるのだろうということを考えます。「愛」という大きな言葉があるからこそ、人は「愛とは何ものなのか」を考え、そのイメージ自体に束縛されていく、というのに似ているとも言える。もっと的確な言葉があれば、人と人の関係も変わるかもしれません。

先にものがあって言葉が付くことと、言葉が先にあってものを考えることの両方があり、その順番は行ったり来たりですが、いつもその「言葉」を外すことで、どんなモノを出来上がるかを考えています。

言葉や名前、意味を外し、自由に空間を構築していったとしても、実際の仕事としてカタチにするには、さまざまな制約があります。空間を恣意的に捉えたとしても、実際に形にするには何をやってもいいわけではありません。無制限に空間づくりを行ってしまっても、自分自身、整理できなくなってしまうので、ある程度の制約があったほうが仕事は進めやすい。何かイメージがあって、それを全方位から捉えようとすると収拾がつかないため、きっかけとして自分でルールをつくります。例えば、そこで何かの「言葉」を新たに用意して整理し、それで削ったり足したりしていくという作業を行います。先の「言葉を外す」作業の逆工程のようなものです。

Q. 整理した空間の中に、どのようにして光や素材といった要素を落とし込んでいくのでしょうか。

文田 素材には、それを使う必然性が高い場合とそうでない場合がありますが、床・壁・天井を区別せず、同じ素材で作りたいと考えた場合、対応できる素材は絞られてきます。例えば、ステンレスなどは使いやすい素材の一つです。実際、ステンレスだけで床・壁・天井をつくった事例もあります。床は荷重や摩擦に耐え得ること、壁や天井は不燃認定がとれているもの、その他、加工性や重量などさまざまな制約があり、自ずと素材は選ばれていくことが少なくありません。

DESIGN PROCESS

デザイン・プロセス

Q.与件に応えるという方法以外に、普段から温めている「いつか実現したいアイデア」が物件と合致した時、具体的な形にするというアプローチもあると思うのですが。

文田　常に素材には興味を持っていて、アイデアをストックしているということはあります。それがうまく仕事につながることもありますし、仕舞い込んで忘れてしまっていたようなことが、プロジェクトの中で引き出されてくる、ということもある。

普段から、特別な素材を扱おうと考えているわけではありません。なぜなら、既存の素材は実績もあり、かつて開発された時は、新しく特別な素材だった。だから、新奇性や希少性などにはこだわらず、ある程度の自由度は持って考えています。時間やコストといった与件によって左右されることはありますが、素材そのものだけでなく、切ったり、貼ったり、曲げたり、削ったりといった加工方法も普段から実験をしていて、そうしたアイデアもストックしています。印象深い素材の使用例としては、日産のショールーム（注1）や「エム・プルミエ」（注2）のカウンター什器で使ったアクリル樹脂系人造大理石があります。通常、人造大理石はカウンタートップなどに用いられますが、そのサンプルを見ている時に、アクリル板ほど軽くなく、石材ほど重くも見えない中庸な素材感であることに気づきました。また、光にかざすと少し透けて見えるという特徴もある。そこで、もっと薄くすれば、より光を透過するんじゃないかと思い、板を削って、3段階に光が透過する板状のものをつくりました。当初、型に流し込んで成型しようと思ったのですが、その時は板状のものしか日本に輸入されておらず、板を重ね、ブロック状にして切削していくという手法を用いました。本来、その素材の用途からすると、透過性はあるべきではなかったのですが、現在では透過性の高い商品も普通に使われています。

Q.色の使い方に関して控えめで、「白」が多用されている印象を受けますが、どのようなお考えからですか。

文田　独立する前と今を比べると、色使いは控えめになっているかもしれません。独立したのがちょうどバブル崩壊の直後で、日本経済全体が落ち込んだ時期でした。どのショップの内装も、あまりコストを掛けることができませんでしたので、素材に頼らないことがコストパフォーマンスを高めるということもありました。

ただ、一方で単純に「白」が好きというのもありました。白は、例えば、壁をスクリーンのように使うなど、光を重視した空間づくりには欠かせない重要なカラーです。学生の頃から、空間の中での「光」という存在に興味があり、当てる光、透過させる光、光によって生まれる影をどう捉えるべきか、といったことを考えていました。一方から光を当てると影ができる。するとその影が邪魔になるから消そうとする。しかし、なかなか影は消せない。であれば、それらも含めた空間をデザインできないか、等々。光に対しての興味は尽きませんでした。そういったことが、「白」を多用する遠因になっているのかもしれません。

それと現実的には、これまで手掛けた物件を見たクライアントから、連鎖反応のように「白い空間を作って欲しい」というオーダーが来るということも、「白」のイメージに繋がっている要因かもしれません。

Q.文田さんの手掛ける空間では、光自体も素材のように捉えられている印象があります。

文田　光は視覚認識できるものの中で、最も不確定な要素と考えています。もちろん、客観的に数値化認識は可能ですが、私たちはそれを実感できない。それを逆手に取り、「光を触感できるとしたら」「光を固めることができたら」など妄想的な仮説に基づいて、「柔らかい光」「ざらざらした光」というように「光を素材化する」ことを考えています。また、形やボリュームを整理する際に、光を介在させることで、より明快に整理できるということも大きいと思います。また、床・壁・天井の考え方と同じなのですが、「光が必要ならダウンライトで照らす」ということを当たり前のように考えてしまうと、ダウンライトが付いている天井の「風景」から逃れられなくなるのではないかと思います。言ってしまえば、ダウンライトも空調の吹き出し口などと同じで、空間構築の中ではあえて欲しいものではない。プリミティブな空間を求めたときには、消したい要素の一つです。それら設備をどうやって造作に組み込んでいくかということを考えています。防災関係の設備は難しいですが、うまく収めていくことには苦慮しています。理想を言えば、出入り口などなく、光も空気も存在してほしいです。〈聞き手 高橋正明〉

注1　自動車メーカー日産の各ギャラリー（P.6〜47）
注2　ブティック「エム・プルミエ」（P.98〜101）

「光を触感できるとしたら」
「光を固めることができたら」など
妄想的な仮説に基づいて、
「柔らかい光」「ざらざらした光」
というように「光を素材化する」
ことを考えています。

NATURAL BODY
NAMBA CITY

Hand Relaxation
NATURAL BODY NAMBA CITY
Namba, Osaka
ナチュラルボディ　なんばCITY店
Completion：April 1999
Total area：112㎡

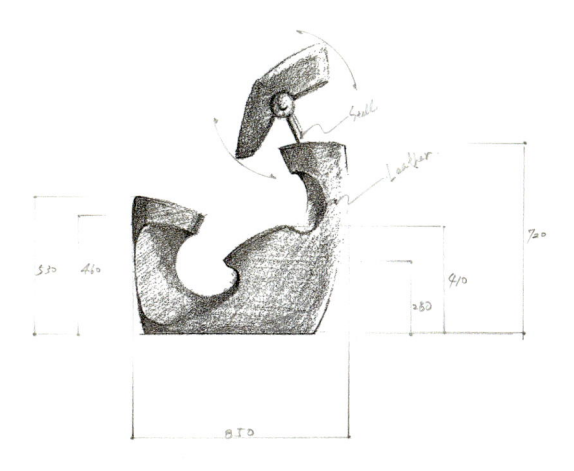

P.72・73上　　　　　施術室
P.73下　　　　　　　エントランスまわり
P.72・73 upper　　　The relaxation room.
P.73 lower　　　　　The entrance.

NATURAL BODY KOBE INTERNATIONAL HOUSE SOL

Hand Relaxation
NATURAL BODY KOBE INTERNATIONAL HOUSE SOL
Chuo-ku, Kobe
ナチュラルボディ　神戸国際会館 SOL店
Completion : April 1999　Total area : 149㎡

P.74 上　　　レセプションカウンターのディテール
P.74 下　　　施術室
P.75　　　　同
P.74 upper　The detail of the reception counter.
P.74 lower　The relaxation room.
P.75　　　　Ditto.

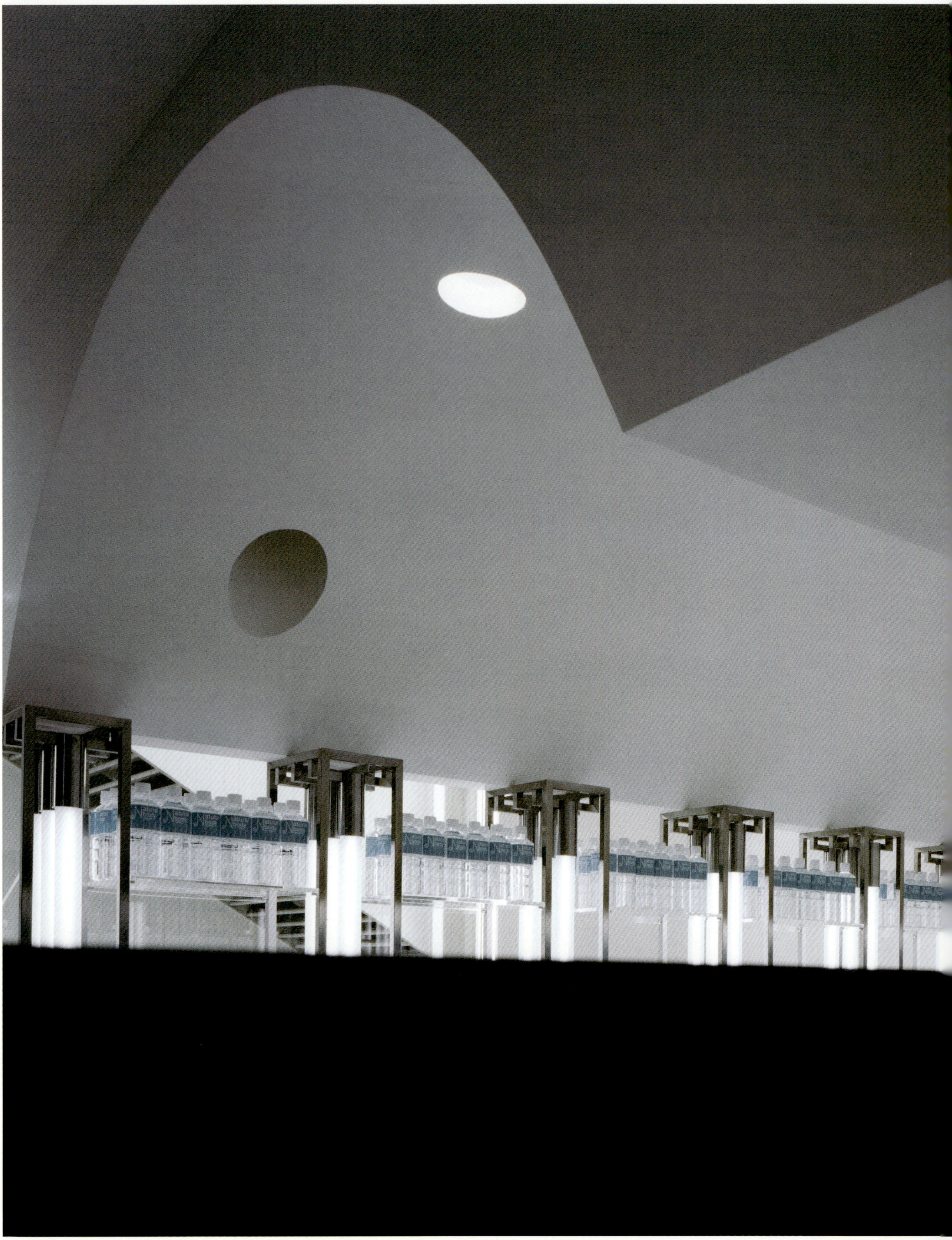

NATURAL BODY SHIBUYA PARCO PART 3

Hand Relaxation
NATURAL BODY SHIBUYA PARCO PART 3
Shibuya, Tokyo
ナチュラルボディ　渋谷PARCO PART 3店
Completion : October 1999　Total area : 83㎡

P.76・77　外部より店内を見る
P.76・77　A view of the interior from the outside.

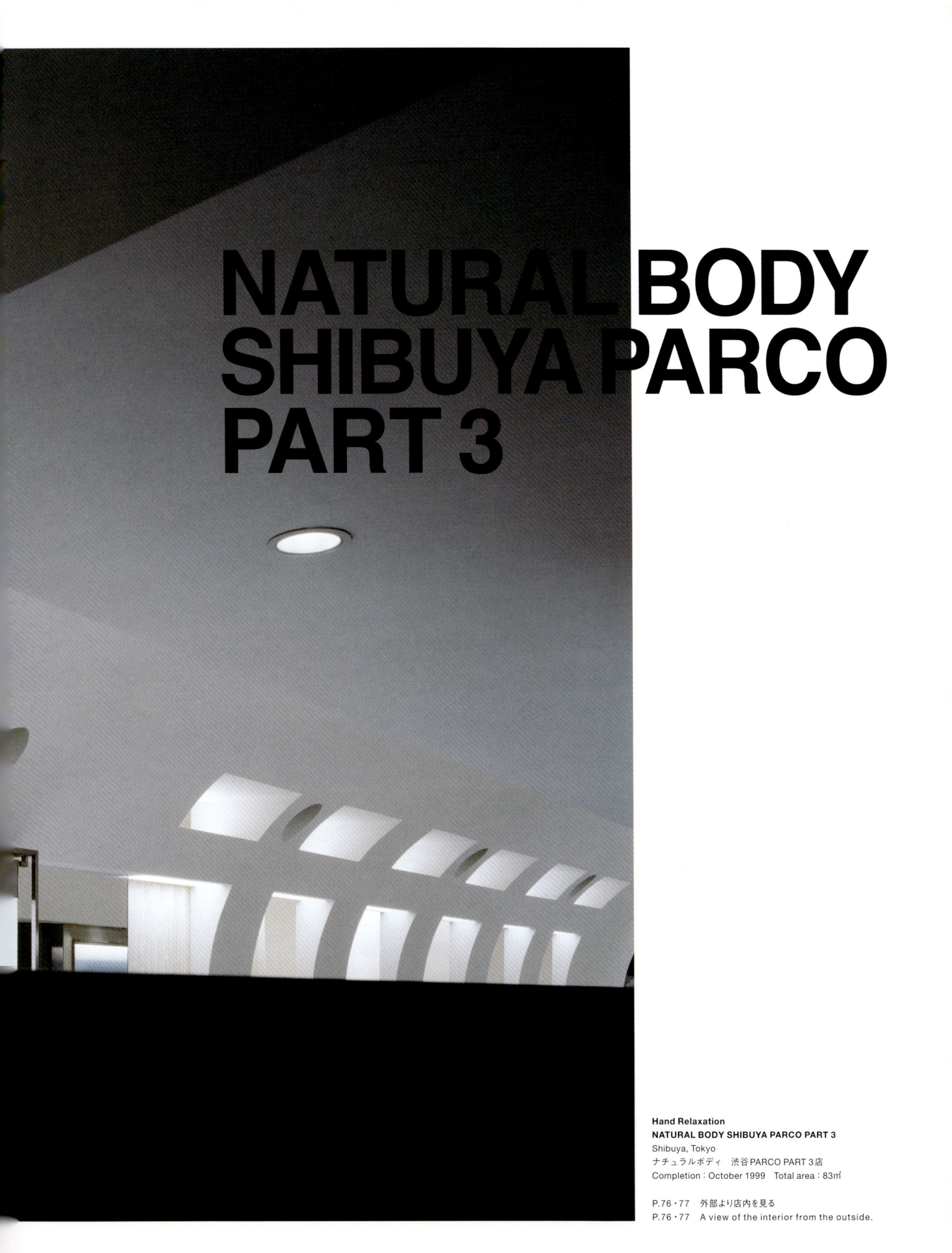

P.78 上　　　施術室内を通る通路
P.78 中　　　施術室
P.78 下　　　ミネラルウオーターのディスプレイケース
P.78・79　　ファサード

P.78 upper　The passage in the relaxation room.
P.78 middle　The relaxation room.
P.78 lower　The display case.
P.78・79　　The facade.

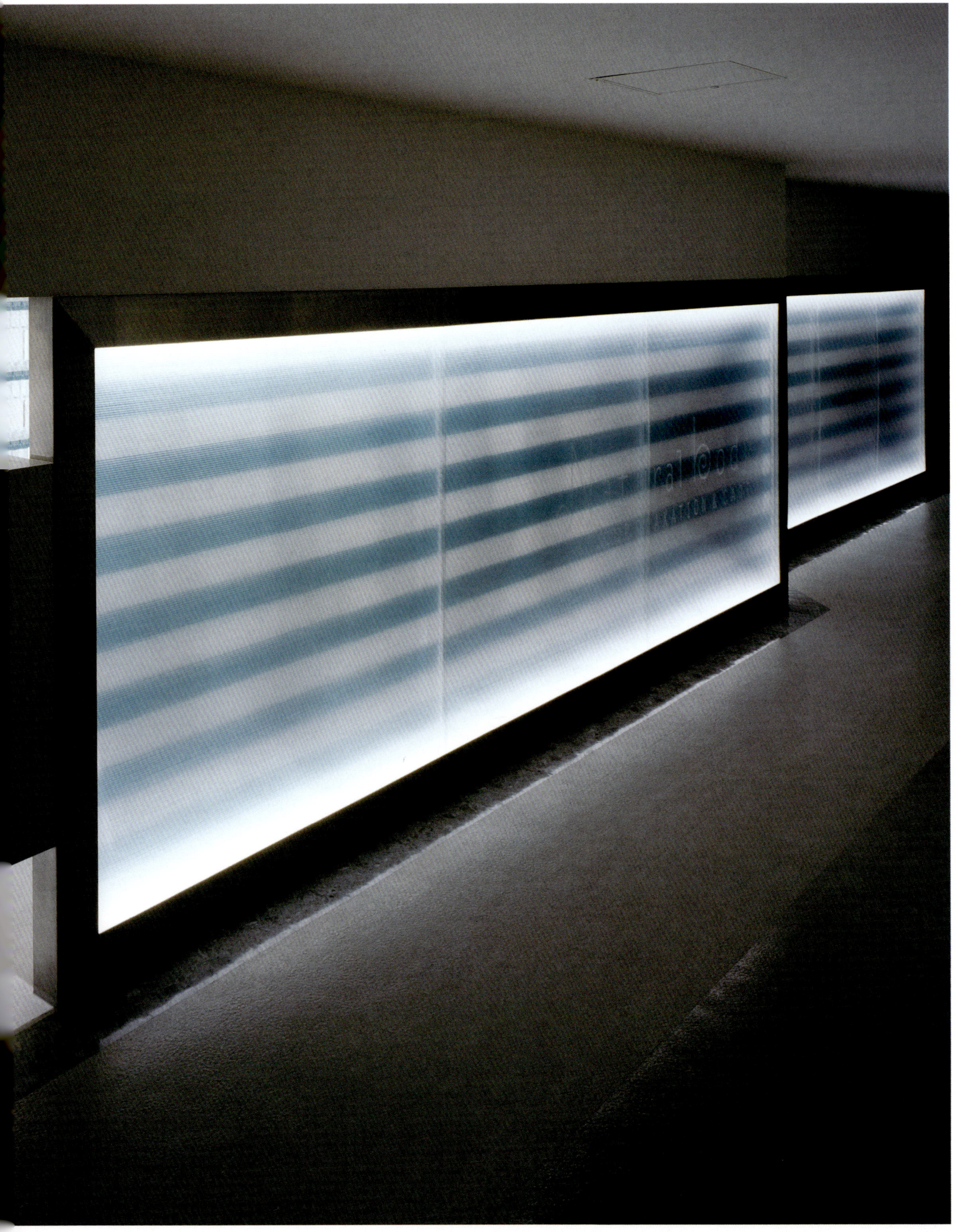

Hand Relaxation
NATURAL BODY HANKYU INTERNATIONAL
Umeda, Osaka
ナチュラルボディ 阪急インターナショナル店
Completion : November 2000　Total area : 109㎡

P.80・81　　　　　施術室天井を見上げる
P.81 左上　　　　施術室
P.81 右上　　　　エントランス
P.81 下　　　　　施術室壁面。曲面天井との設置部に間接光
P.80・81　　　　　A look up at the ceiling of the relaxation room.
P.81 upper left　 The relaxation room.
P.81 upper right The entrance.
P.81 lower　　　 The wall in the relaxation room.

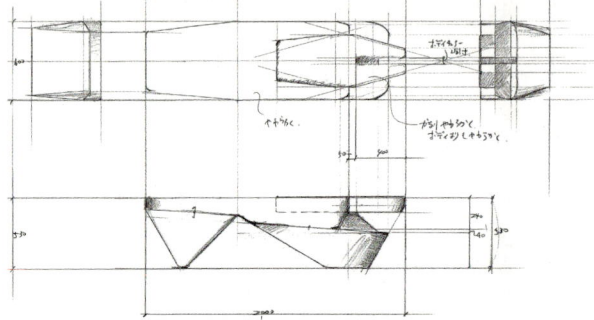

NATURAL BODY HANKYU INTERNATIONAL

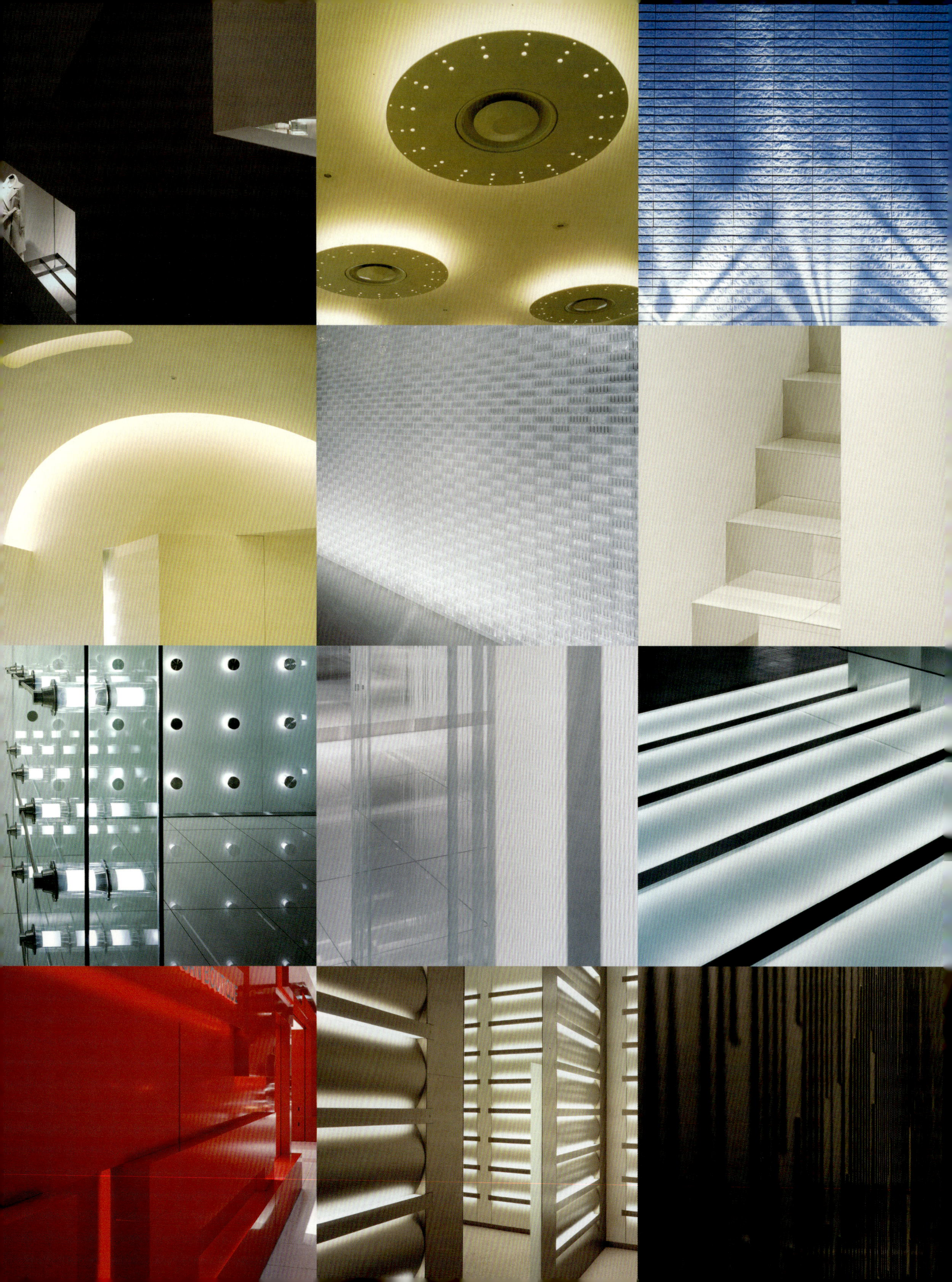

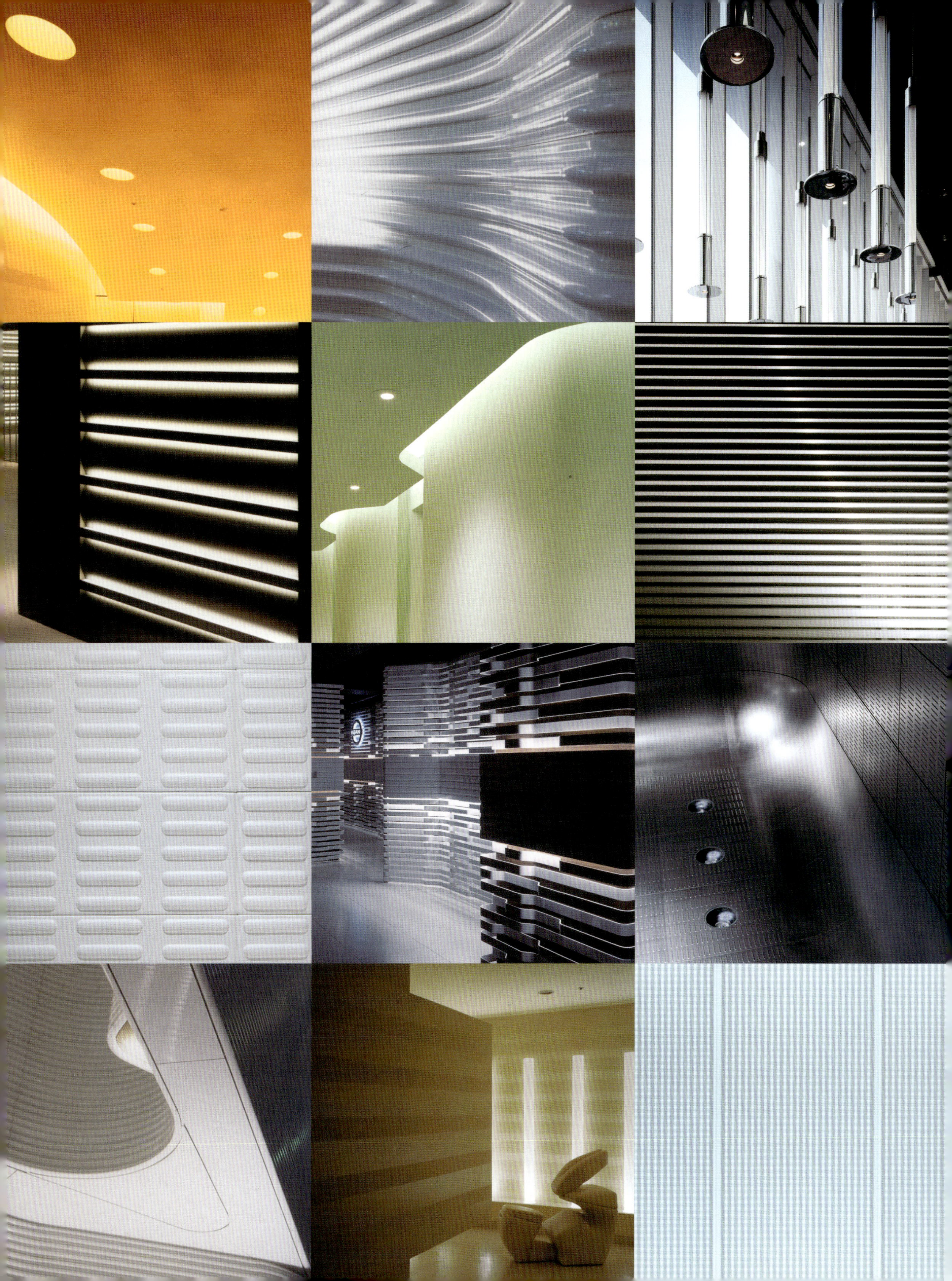

M,I,D, SHOP
UMEDA HANKYU

Boutique
M,I,D, SHOP UMEDA HANKYU
Umeda, Osaka
エム・アイ・ディーショップ 阪急うめだ店
Completion : September 2003   Total area : 142㎡

P.84 　コーナー部分。ハンガー什器は
　　　　ガラス壁面側に固定されている
P.85 上　クリアブロック積みスクリーンのディテール
P.85 下　店内全景
P.84 　　The corner of the shop.
P.85 上　The wall of piled-up clear blocks.
P.85 下　The interior.

P.86 上　　　　エントランスまわり
P.86 下　　　　ショップフロント
P.87　　　　　 フィッティングルーム
P.86 upper　　The entrance.
P.86 lower　　The facade.
P.87　　　　　 The fitting room.

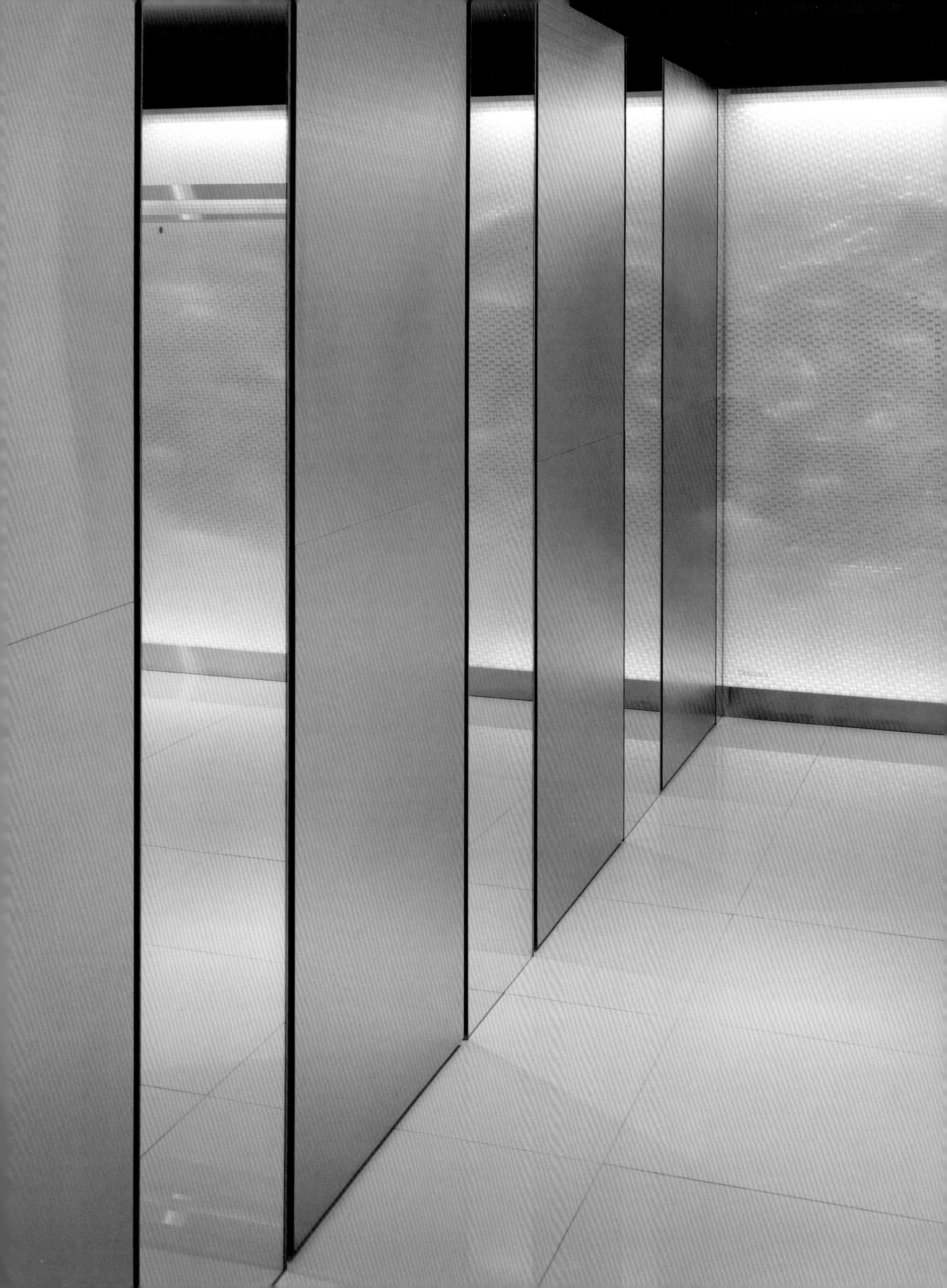
Diablock

Boutique
M,I,D, SHOP YURAKUCHO HANKYU
Yurakucho, Tokyo
エム・アイ・ディー ショップ 有楽町阪急店
Completion : September 2003　Total area : 154㎡

P.88 上　　　棚什器越しにレジカウンター方向を見る
P.88 中　　　店内全景
P.88 下　　　エントランスまわり
P.88・89　　ショップウオール越しに店内を見る
P.88 upper　The checkout counter.
P.88 middle　The interior.
P.88 lower　The entrance.
P.88・89　　The interior over the shop wall.

M,I,D, SHOP YURAKUCHO HANKYU

M,I,D, PRESS ROOM

Pressroom
M,I,D, PRESS ROOM
Omotesando, Tokyo
エム・アイ・ディー プレスルーム
Completion : December 2004
Total area : 358㎡／B1F・196㎡　B2F・162㎡

P.90　外部から店内を見る
P.91　階段室越しにエントランス方向を見返す。
　　　二重ガラスにはアルミダイキャスト製の
　　　オリジナル照明器具が規則正しくはめ込まれている
P.90　A view of the interior from outside.
P.91　The entrance over the stairway.

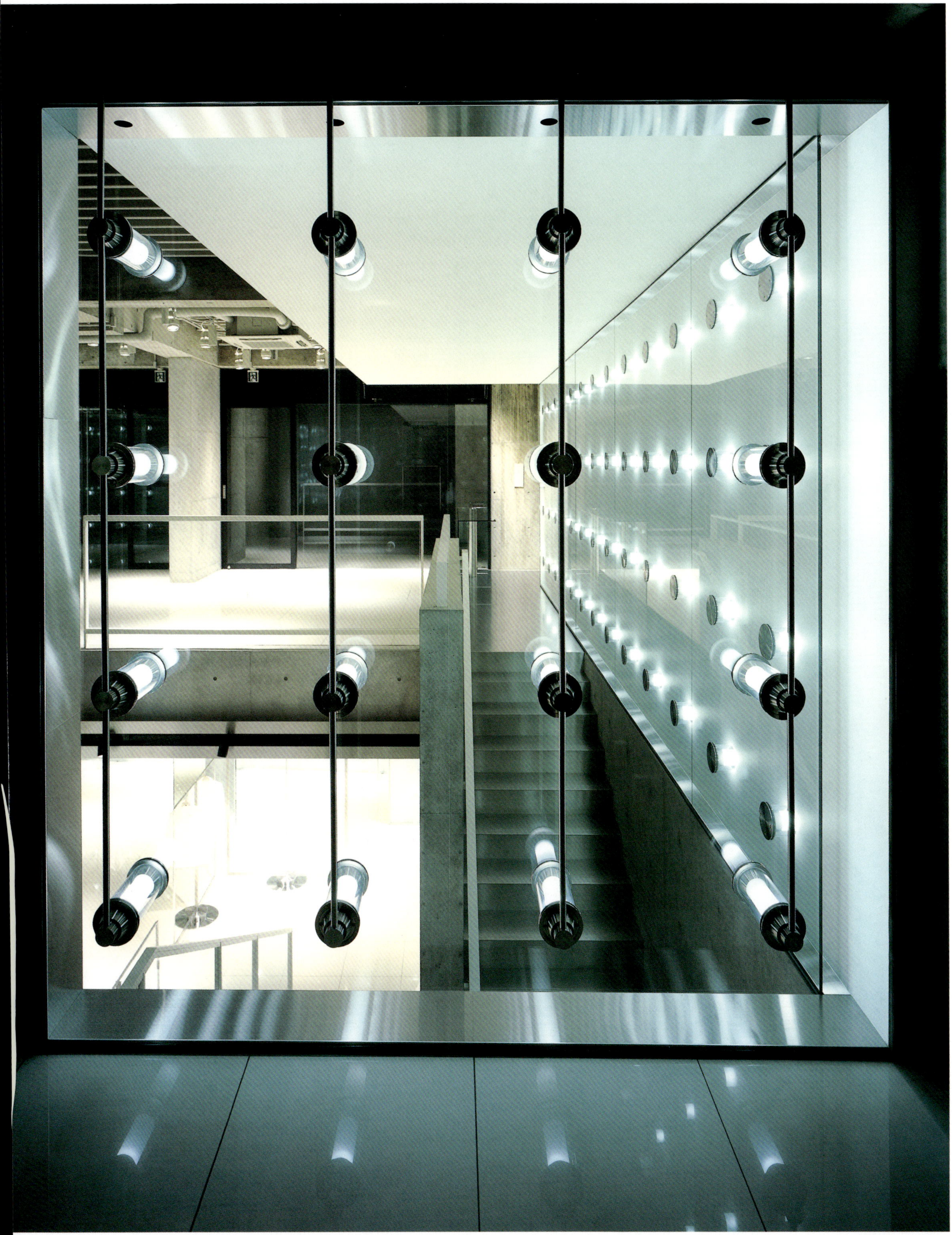

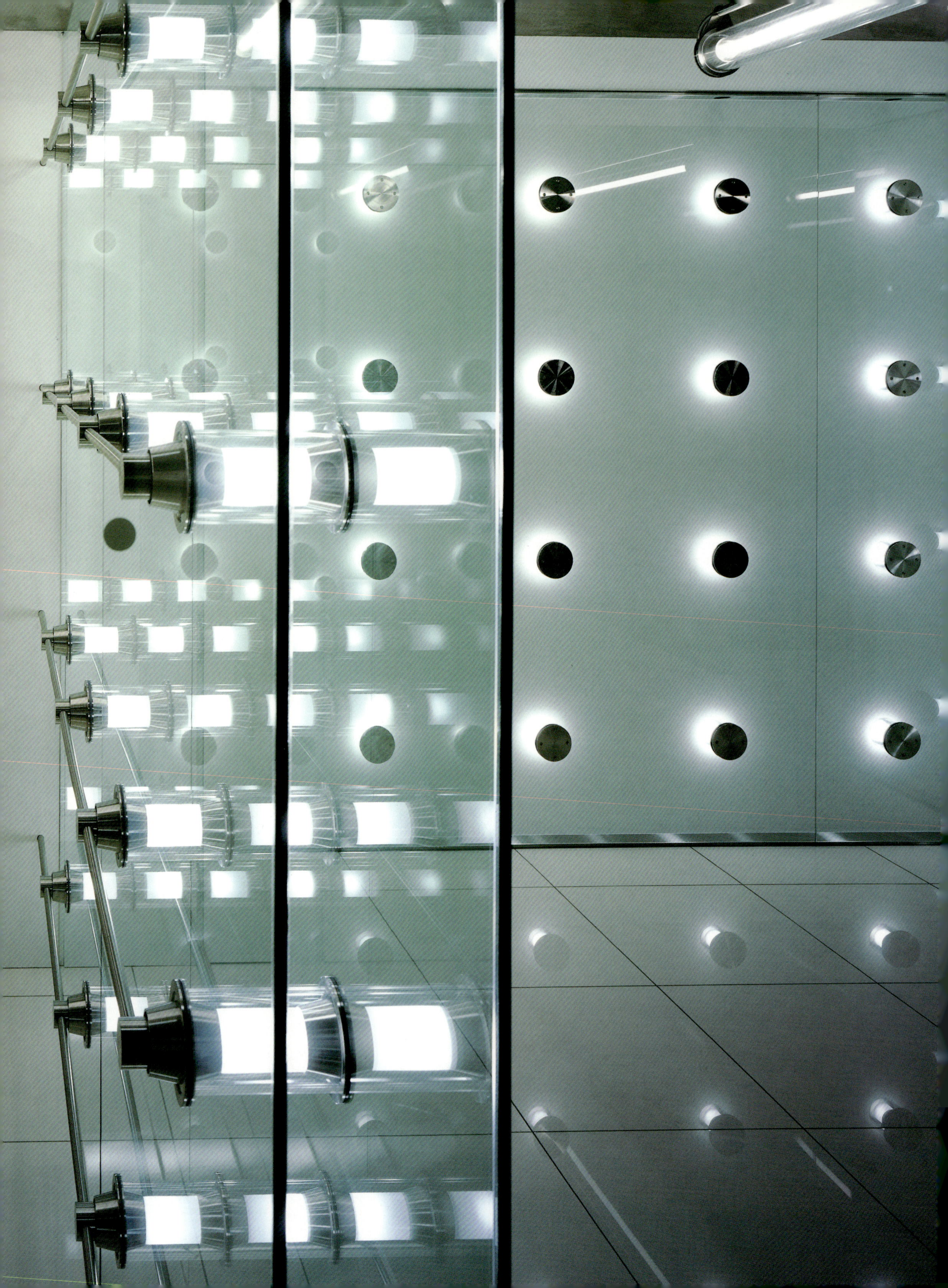

P.92 照明器具のディテール
P.93 プレスオフィス全景
P.92 Detail of the illuminator.
P.93 A view of the entire press office.

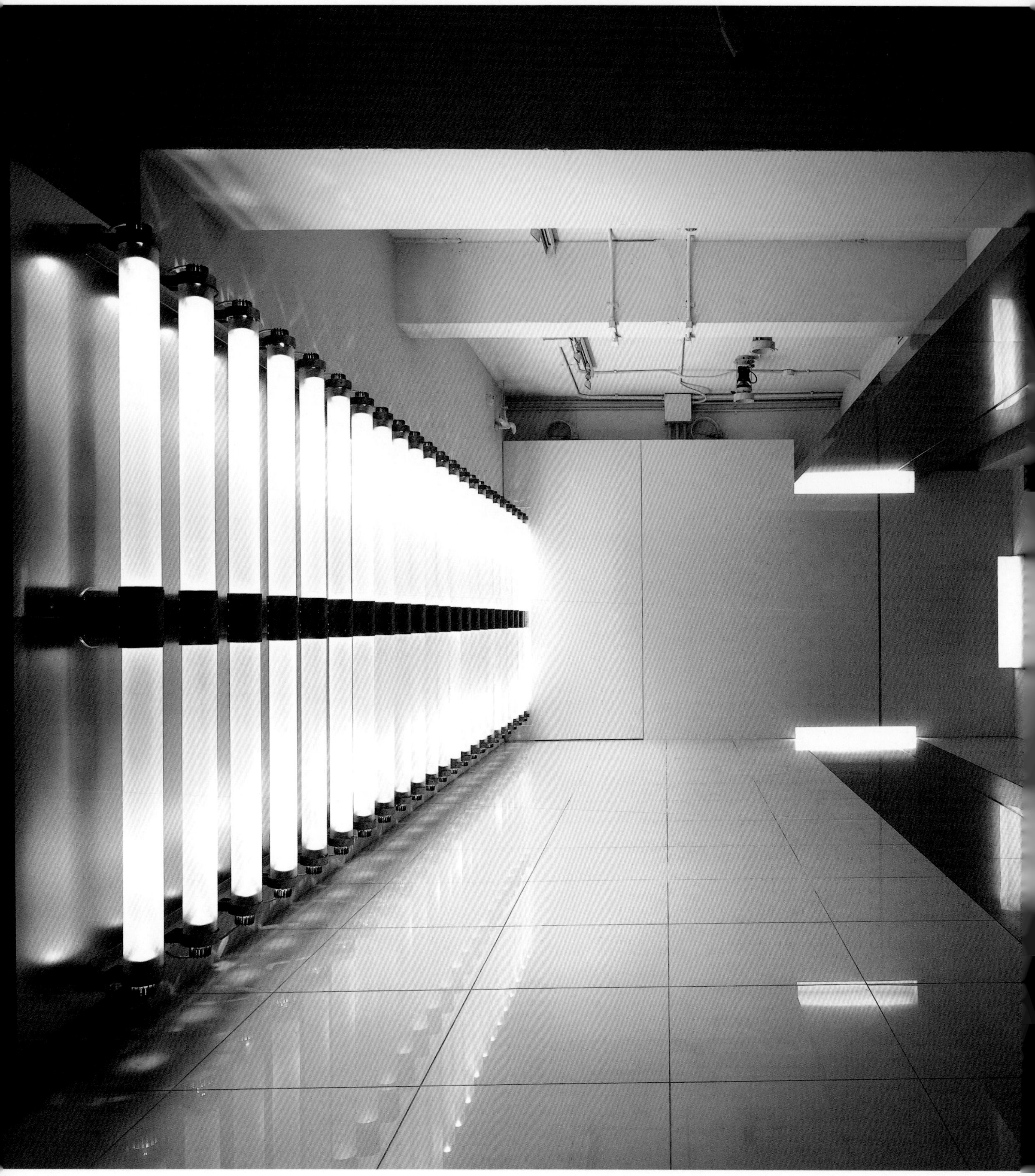

M,I,D, HEAD QUARTERS

Office
M,I,D, HEADQUARTERS
Honmachi, Osaka
エム・アイ・ディー 本社
Completion：July 2004
Total area：97㎡／1F・58㎡　2F・38㎡

P.94・95　壁面に円柱状の照明器具が
　　　　　等間隔に並ぶ1階プレスルーム
P.95　　　エントランスから1階プレスルームと
　　　　　2階のオフィスへ続く螺旋階段を見る
P.94・95　The press room on the first floor.
P.95　　　The entrance.

m-i-d

M,I,D, HEAD QUARTERS ANNEX

Office
M,I,D, HEADQUARTERS ANNEX
Honmachi, Osaka
エム・アイ・ディー 本社アネックス
Completion：July 2004

P.96	アルミルーバーで囲われた外装のディテール
P.97 上	外見全景。移動する視点で表情が変化するようルーバーを構成
P.97 下	前面道路越しに見る
P.96	Detail of the exterior.
P.97 upper・lower	The exterior.

M-PREMIER

SHIJOKAWARAMACHI HANKYU STORE

Boutique
M-PREMIER SHIJOKAWARAMACHI HANKYU STORE
Shijokawaramachi, Kyoto
エム・プルミエ　四条河原町阪急店
Completion：September 2003　Total area：213㎡

P.98・99　　外部より店内を見る
P.99 上　　ハンガー什器を設置した壁面
P.99 下　　ショーウインドー越しに店内を見る
P.98・99　　A view of the interior from outside.
P.99 upper　The wall in the shop.
P.99 lower　The interior over the show window.

Boutique
**M-PREMIER TENMAYA
HIROSHIMA HACCHOBORI STORE**
Hacchobori, Hiroshima
エム・プルミエ　天満屋広島八丁堀店
Completion：March 2004
Total area：199㎡

P.100 上	ショップフロント
P.100 左下	什器越しに店内を見る
P.100 右下	店舗のキーアイコンとなっている ランダムストライプ
P.101	ミラーとストライプが混じり合う壁面
P.100 upper	The entrance.
P.100 lower left	The interior.
P.100 lower right	The Random Stripes that are a key icon of the shop.
P.101	Wall that mixes mirrors with stripes.

M-PREMIER TENMAYA HIROSHIMA HACCHOBORI STORE

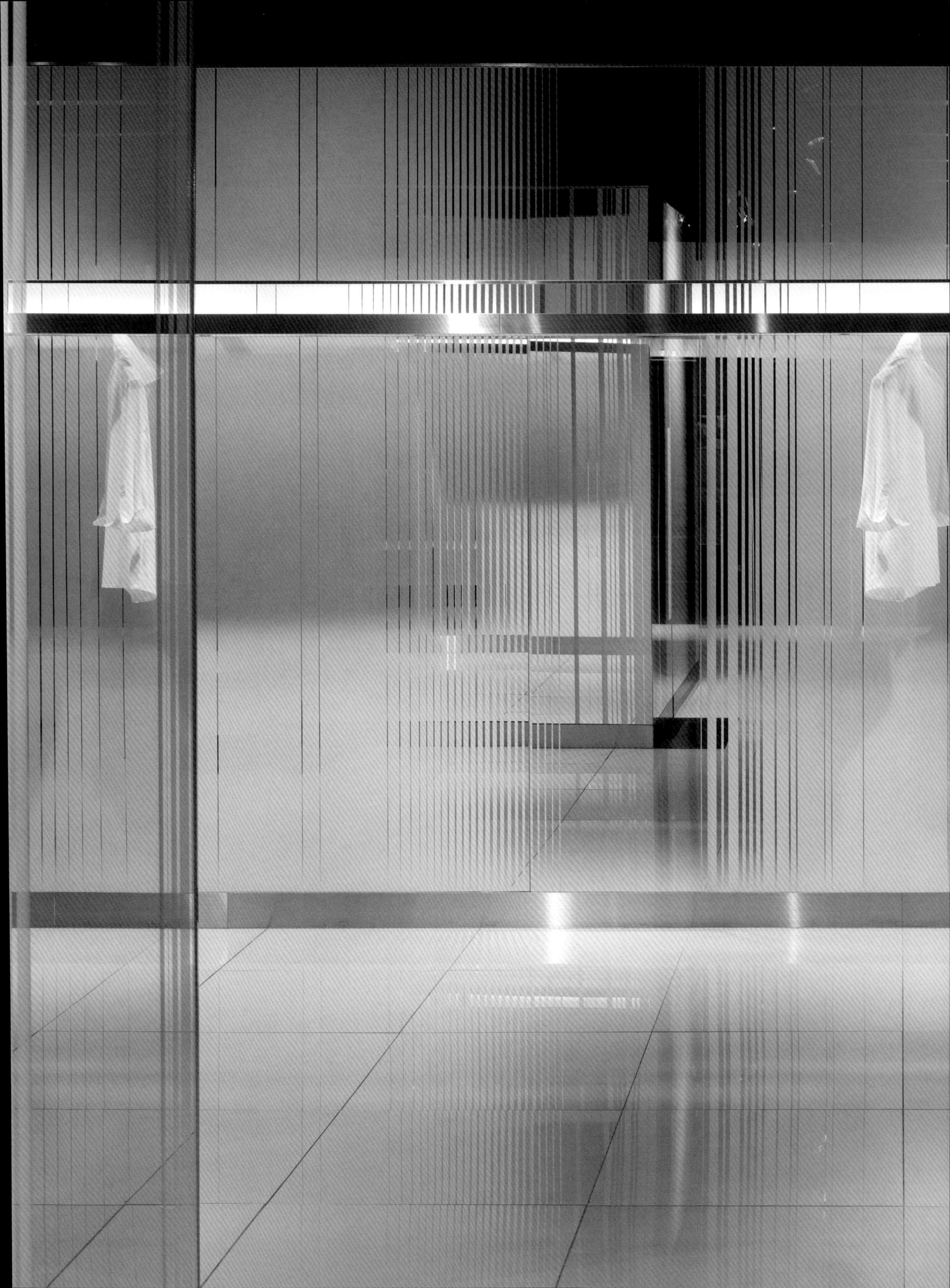

TRE PINI

Boutique
TRE PINI
Nishi-ku, Kobe
トレピニ
Completion : March 1998
Total area : 55㎡

P.102・103 　内照式のルーバー壁面から光が漏れるコーナー。
　　　　　　スリットにはめ込む什器パーツは、
　　　　　　内部に収納が可能
P.103 上　　ガラス製ディスプレイ什器
P.103 下　　可動するエントランス壁面
P.102・103　The display wall.
P.103 upper　The display shelf made of glass.
P.103 lower　The entrance.

ETE
AOYAMA

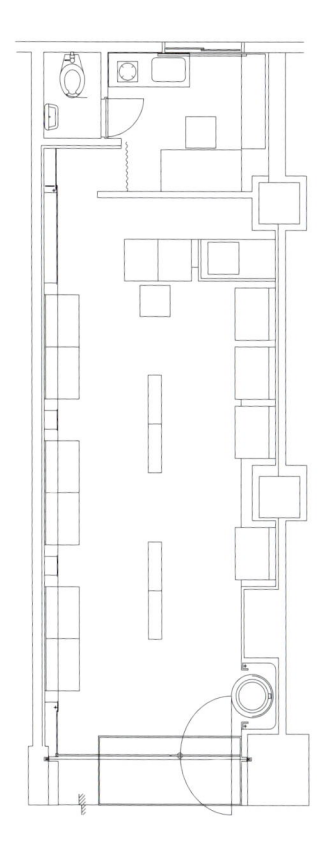

Accessory Shop
ETE AOYAMA
Minamiaoyama, Tokyo
エテ　青山本店
Completion : May 2000
Total area : 36㎡

P.104　　　外部から店内を見る
P.105 上　　店内全景
P.105 下　　地面から浮き上がったような壁面什器
P.104　　　A view of the interior from outside.
P.105 upper　A view of the entire shop.
P.105 lower　Wall showcase.

Accessory Shop
ETE+ NAGOYA LACHIC
Nagoya, Aichi
エテ・プラス　名古屋ラシック店
Completion : February 2006　　Total area : 52㎡

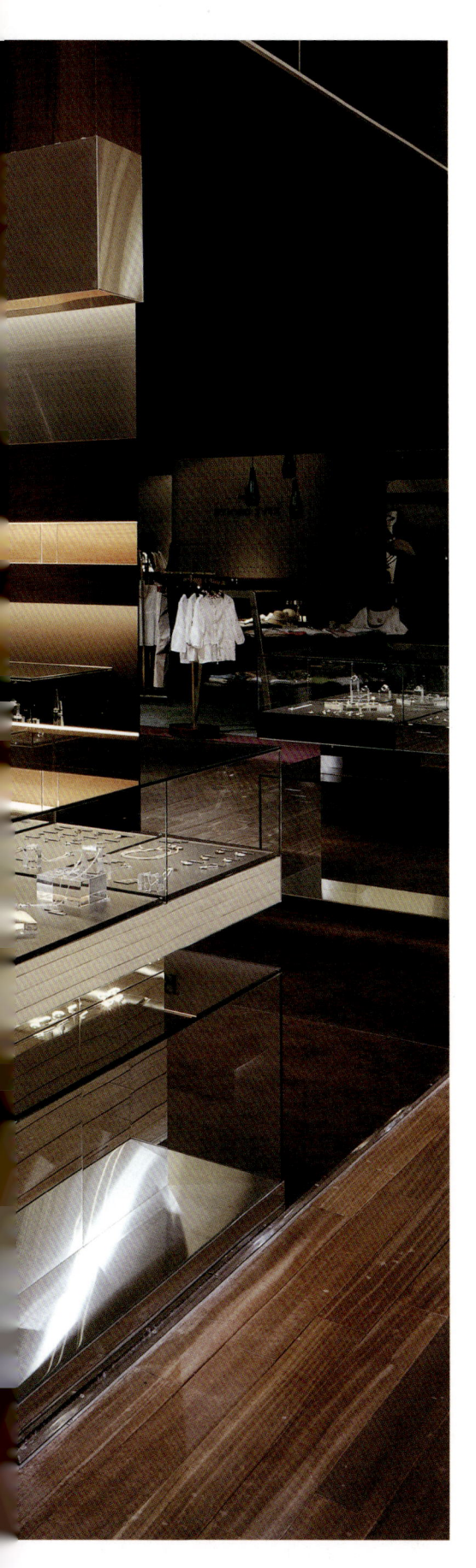

P.106・107　店内全景
P.107　　　壁面に構成された什器群
P.106・107　A view of the entire shop.
P.107　　　Wall showcase.

ETE+ NAGOYA LACHIC

THE SUPER SUITS STORE AWAJICHO

Boutique
THE SUPER SUITS STORE AWAJICHO
Awajicho, Tokyo
ザ・スーパースーツストア　淡路町店

Completion : December 2004　Total area : 249㎡

P.108 上　　　外部から店内を見る。重厚感を与える赤を多用
P.108 下　　　身長別に配置されたスーツラック
P.109 左　　　什器構成
P.109 右　　　壁面に並ぶステンレス製ラック
P.109 下　　　サイズと柄で分類されるシャツ専用ラック
P.108 upper　A view of the interior from the outside.
P.108 lower　The suit rack in the shop.
P.109 left　　The display wall.
P.109 right　The rack made of stainless steel.
P.109 lower　The shelf for shirt.

ABITO NERO

NECK
41
SHIRT 38 39 40 41 42 43
REGULAR &
LONG SLEEVE
¥2,900 (in tax ¥3,045)
¥3,800 (in tax ¥3,990)
NECK
42
NECK
43

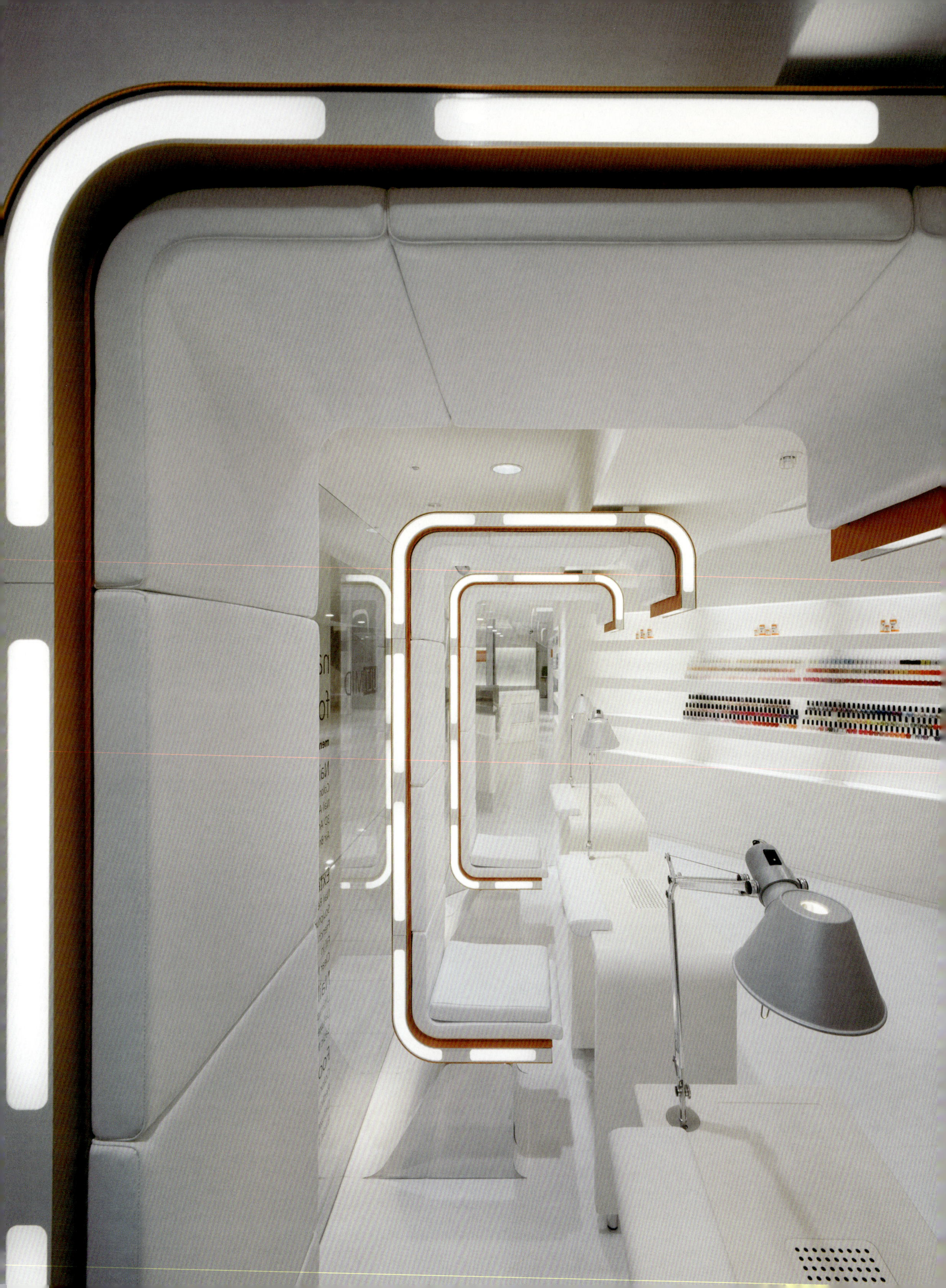

OSAKA TAKASHIMAYA ROOM IN BLOOM

Boutique & Common Space
OSAKA TAKASHIMAYA ROOM IN BLOOM
Namba, Osaka
ルームインブルーム 大阪髙島屋
Completion : March 2002
Total area : 1150㎡

P.110	ビューティーゾーンのネイルサロンブースを通して見る。この複合ショップは、他にファッション、カフェ&カルチャーの計3業態(ゾーン)で構成される
P.111 左上	カフェ
P.111 右上	レジカウンター
P.111 左下	ファッションコーナー
P.111 右下	外部から見た店内
P.110	A view of the booth of the nail salon.
P.111 upper left	The cafe.
P.111 upper right	The checkout counter.
P.111 lower left	The fashion corner.
P.111 lower right	A view of the interior from outside.

INTERVIEW 2

DESIGN ROOTS
デザイン・ルーツ

Q.学生時代は建築史もお好きだったそうですが、どこに興味をもたれたのでしょうか。
文田 芸術やデザインについての知識はまったく無いに等しかったですね。ですから、とにかく身近にある本をかたっぱしから読んでいました。当時は、例えば芸術の独創性について、「個人の内面から出てくる情緒的なものだろう」ぐらいにしか考えていませんでした。しかし学んでいくにしたがって、その時代ごとの「科学的発見」と「芸術表現」というものはとても密接にリンクしているんだということに気づき、興味がどんどん深くなっていきました。そうした芸術のダイナミズムのようなものに感動し、芸術とは生まれるべくして生まれているのだなと感じたことが、今でも鮮明に記憶に残っています。

Q.文田さんのデザインには、そうした「時代とリンクしている」という印象も持たせながら、古びないところがあるように感じます。
文田 時代によって受け入れてもらえるものと、そうでないものがあるのは事実でしょう。その時々で求められるものは変わっていきます。数年前までステンレス素材を使った表現を多く用いましたが、学校を卒業してすぐの頃にも同じようなチャレンジはしていました。しかし当時は、デザインに「温かみ」が求められている時代で、今のようには受け入れられませんでした。単純に、木や土は温かい、金属は冷たいというような共通認識が時代を経て、変容していったのだと思います。

Q.「日本的なもの」にこだわったりはするのでしょうか。
文田 もちろん「日本的なもの」というのは私にとって大きな命題です。私が学生の頃にもジャポネスクブームがあって、江戸とか京都といった文化が欧米にもてはやされていた時期がありました。音楽の世界では、YMO（イエロー・マジック・オーケストラ）が欧米でも認められた頃で、言葉の壁を越えたインストゥルメンタルでの表現は、非常にコンテンポラリーに「日本的なもの」、あるいは「アジア的なもの」を伝えていたと思います。
一方空間表現は、言葉の壁がないので、色や形、素材、光でそのまま伝えることができる。その中で、自分自身が考える「コンテンポラリー」を日本的なるもので表現していきたいと思っています。
今までの仕事で言えば、「日産銀座ギャラリー」（P.22）で、グローバル企業である日産が「日本の企業であること」を、直接的な表現ではなく、DNAレベルで伝えらるようなデザインをしてほしいと求められました。もちろん、そのまま「日本」を表現しても、和風にしかならない、ということはクライアントとの共通認識でした。そういう言葉は使わずに、コンテンポラリーなデザインをしていったのですが、後からクライアントに「内照式の人造大理石は、障子から拡散された光のようだ」とか、「外壁の波打ったディテールは、禅寺の庭の模様のようだ」と解釈することができる、という感想を聞いたときはうれしかったですね。そういった多様な解釈が出てくるほうが面白いと思います。
日本的なるものの表現として、日本古来の周知の建築言語や比喩（江戸、京都、風呂

敷、襖など）を用いていることを声高に謳う事例に出会うと失笑してしまうことがあります。それはおそらく、それらの表現が既にジャポネスク的な日本の表現として一般化してしまっていて、隠喩のつもりが直喩として伝わってしまうからではないかと思います。

手垢のついた方法から脱すべきと考え模索していた私にとって、「DNAレベルでの日本の表現」という言葉はとても良いヒントになりました。感覚を表す言葉が見つかった、という感じです。そのDNAレベルでの表現という感覚は、視覚的に表出はしていなくとも、空間表現に確実に作用して、読み取ることができる存在になるものと解釈しています。

Q.大阪のご出身ですが、ものづくりを触発するような環境だったのですか。

文田　私が育ったのは、東大阪の町工場が多く集まる地域の近くです。子供の頃の遊び場と言えば、錆びたトタン壁に囲まれた工場界隈で、うろうろしては廃棄してあるボルトやナット、バネ、何かの部品などを拾い集めて、密かに喜んでいました。プラモデルなども作っては分解し、好きな部分だけ残しておいてそれをまた組み合わせたりして遊んでいましたね。父が大工だったので、工作道具には不自由しませんでした。そうした経験や記憶が影響しているのかわかりませんが、やはり今でも見た目がマッシブであったり、メカニックであったり、攻撃的な形状のものに何故か惹かれます。こういうことを言うと、割と他人にネガティブに捉えられがちなので、今では、一つひとつのスケールを小さくしたり、威圧感を抑え

たりしています（笑）。抑圧することで見つけることができるアイデアや結果もありますし、機会があれば解放することもあります。

Q.仕事はどのような流れで進めるのでしょうか。

文田　基本的には、依頼が来て初めて仕事が始まるわけですが、依頼は人のご紹介もありますし、私がデザインをした店を実際に見て、直接訪ねてきてくれる方もいます。初めてのクライアントの場合は、まずやりたいことをすべて聞き出し、コンセプトが抽象的にならないように軌道修正しつつ、彼らの考えていることを形と自分の言葉に置き換えながら整理していきます。その段階で、クライアントの中に混在しているイメージのズレなどをなくしていきながら、同時に平面プランで実質的な機能を確認していき、最終的に3DCGとマテリアルでプレゼンします。模型は、求められたりクライアントの好みで用意することもありますが、基本的にはつくりません。建築のプレゼンなどでは模型は有効とも思いますが、インテリアでは空間の中に入った感覚が大事なので、3DCGの方が体験感を伝えやすいからです。

一方で、私の仕事のやり方を気に入っていただいて、長年一緒に仕事をしているクライアントもいます。そうしたクライアントからはたまに「文田らしくないものをつくってくれ」と言われることもあります。それはなかなか難しい注文ですが、抑圧することで新しいものを見つけ出せるかもしれない期待感は生まれます。しかし結局のところ、私がデザインするものは、私以外のものにはならないのですが。　〈聞き手 高橋正明〉

空間表現は、言葉の壁がないので、
色や形、素材、光でそのまま伝えることができる。
その中で、自分自身が考える「コンテンポラリー」を
日本的なるもので表現していきたい。

SPIRITUAL MODE
MINAMI AOYAMA

Showroom
SPIRITUAL MODE MINAMIAOYAMA
Minamiaoyama, Tokyo
スピリチュアルモード 南青山
Completion : November 2005
Total area : 289㎡ ／ B1F・272㎡　1F・17㎡

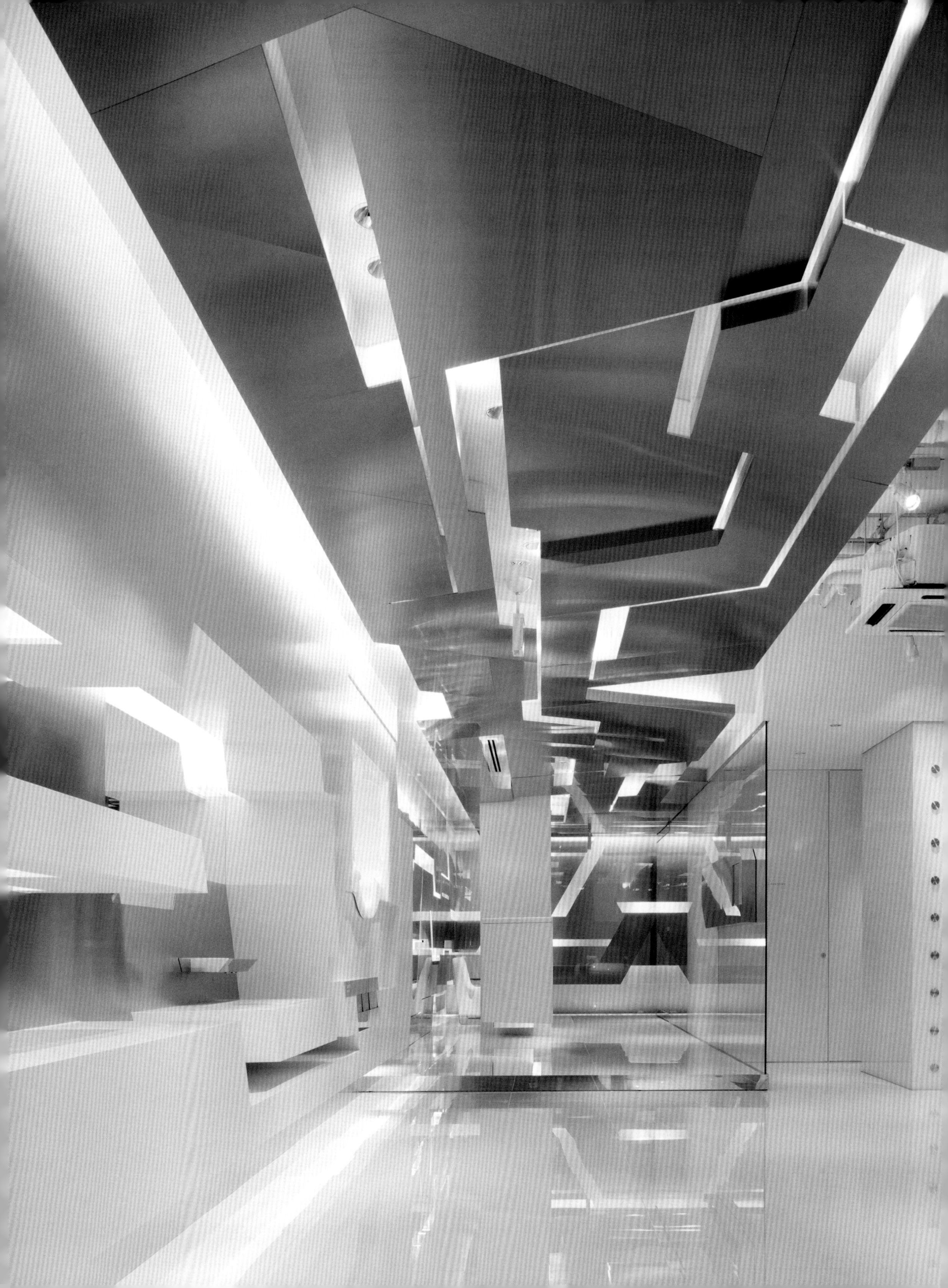

SPIRITUAL MODE

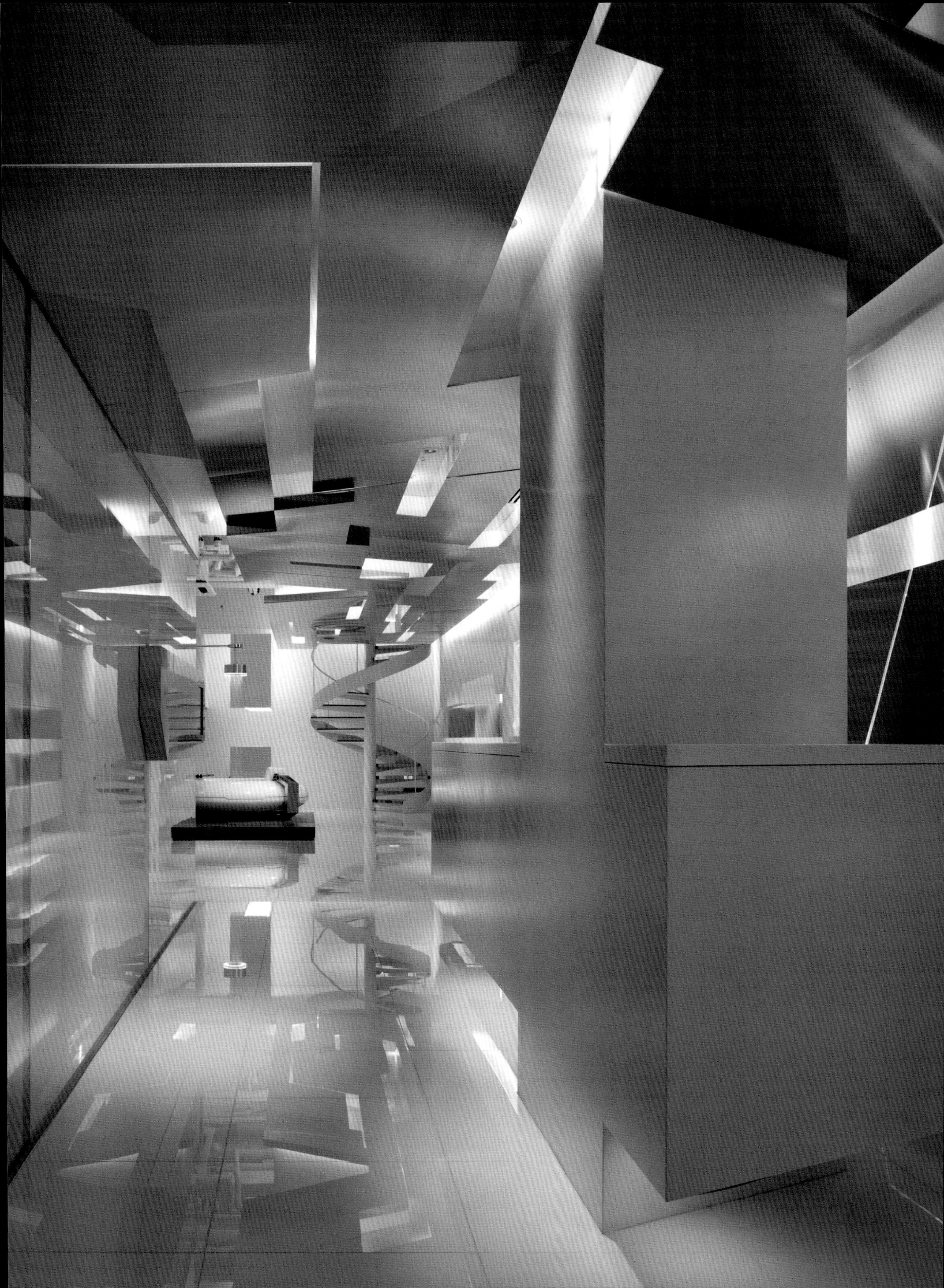

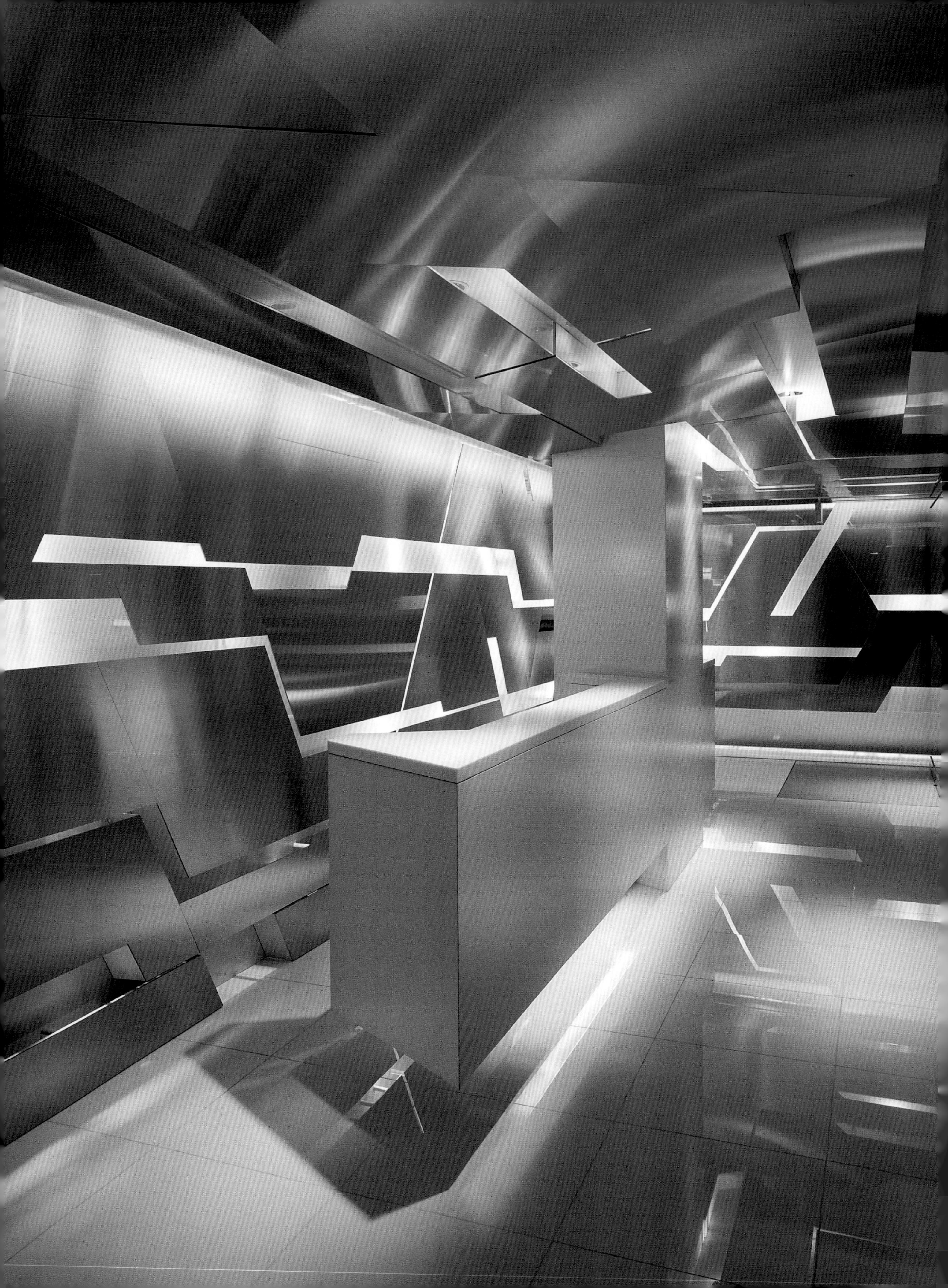

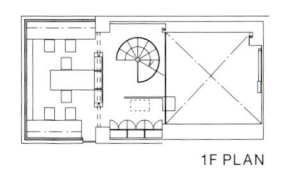

P.114	地下1階メーンエントランスのレセプションエリア
P.115	レセプション方向を見返す
P.116	1階と吹き抜けになった店奥
P.117	レセプション側から店奥を見通す
P.118	レセプションカウンター
P.119 上下	ユニットバス用の個室ブース
P.114	The entrance.
P.115	A view of the reception.
P.116	The display space on the first floor.
P.117	A view of the display space on the first floor.
P.118	The reception counter.
P.119 upper・lower	The booth for modular bath.

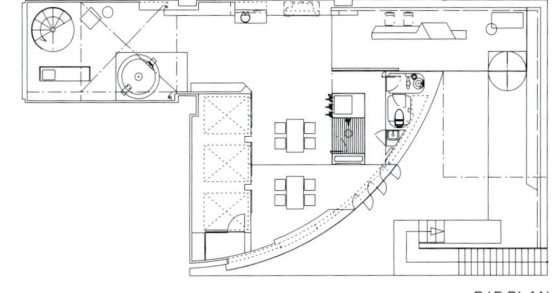

1F PLAN

B1F PLAN

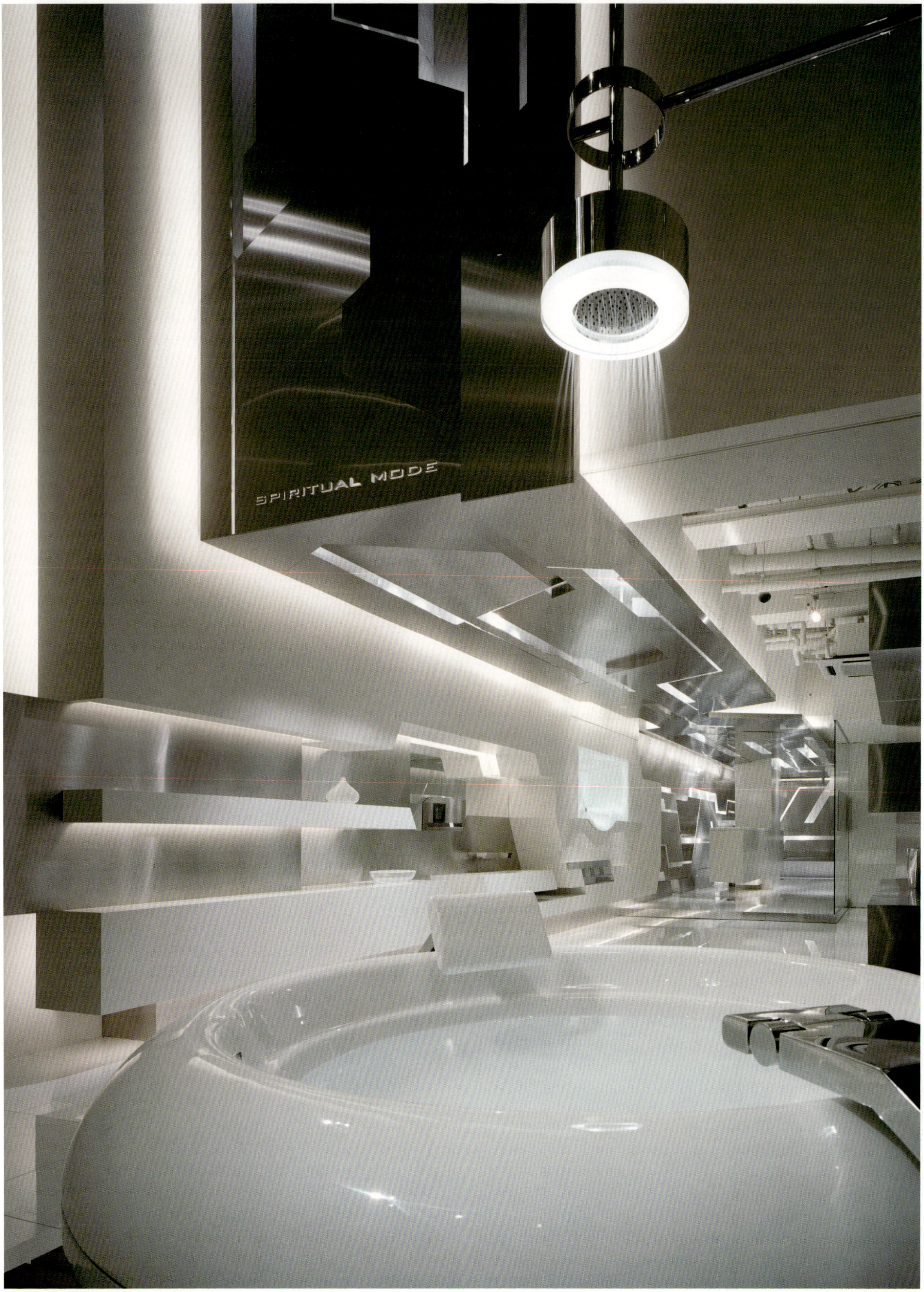
SPIRITUAL MODE

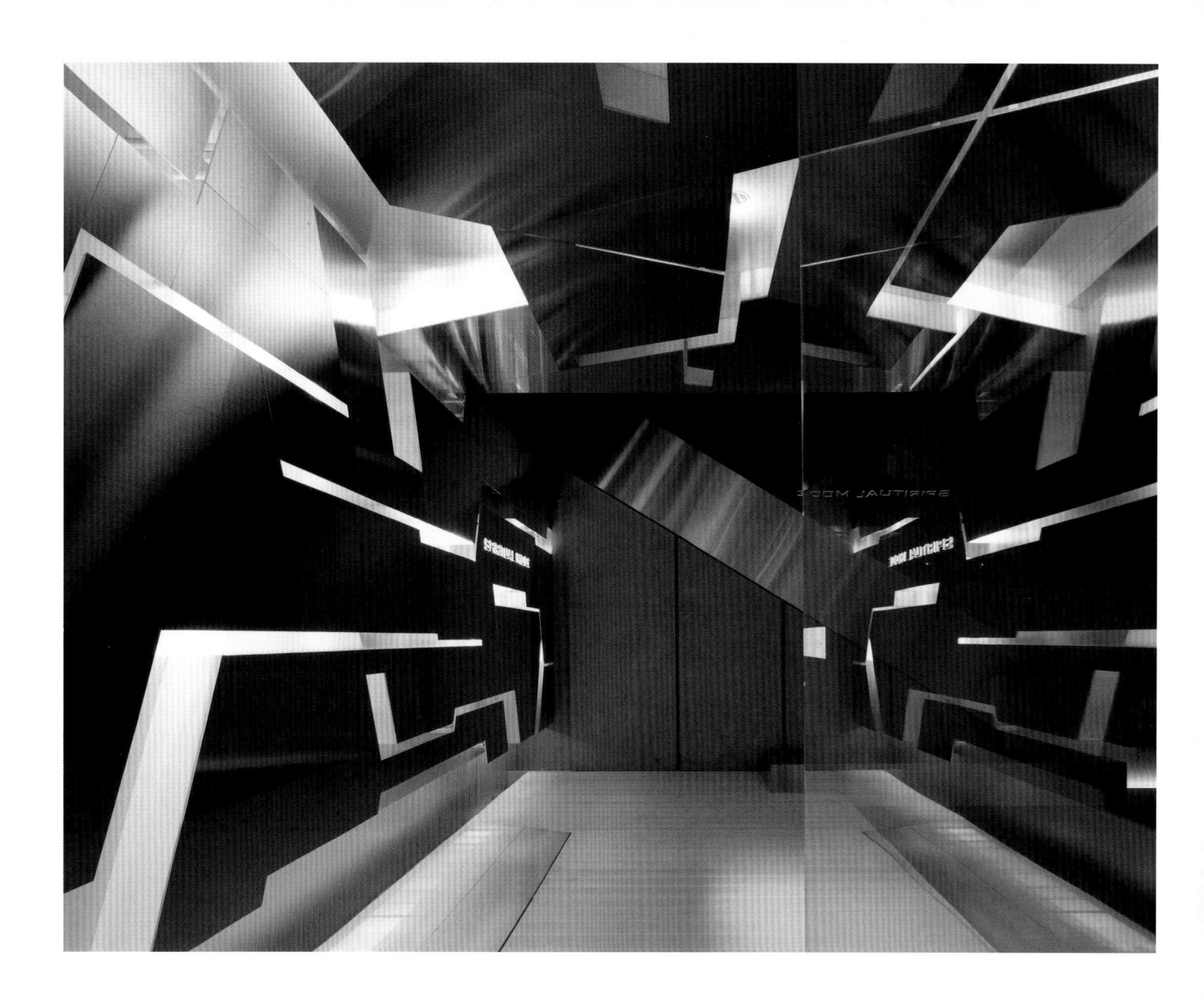

P.120	手前の円形バスタブは文田のオリジナルデザイン
P.121 上	ヘキサゴン（六角形）を分解、再構成したステンレス製壁面
P.121 下	エントランスまわり
P.120	The display space on the first underground floor.
P.121 upper	The detail of the stainless wall.
P.121 lower	The entrance.

SPIRITUAL MODE KYOTO

SPIRITUAL MODE

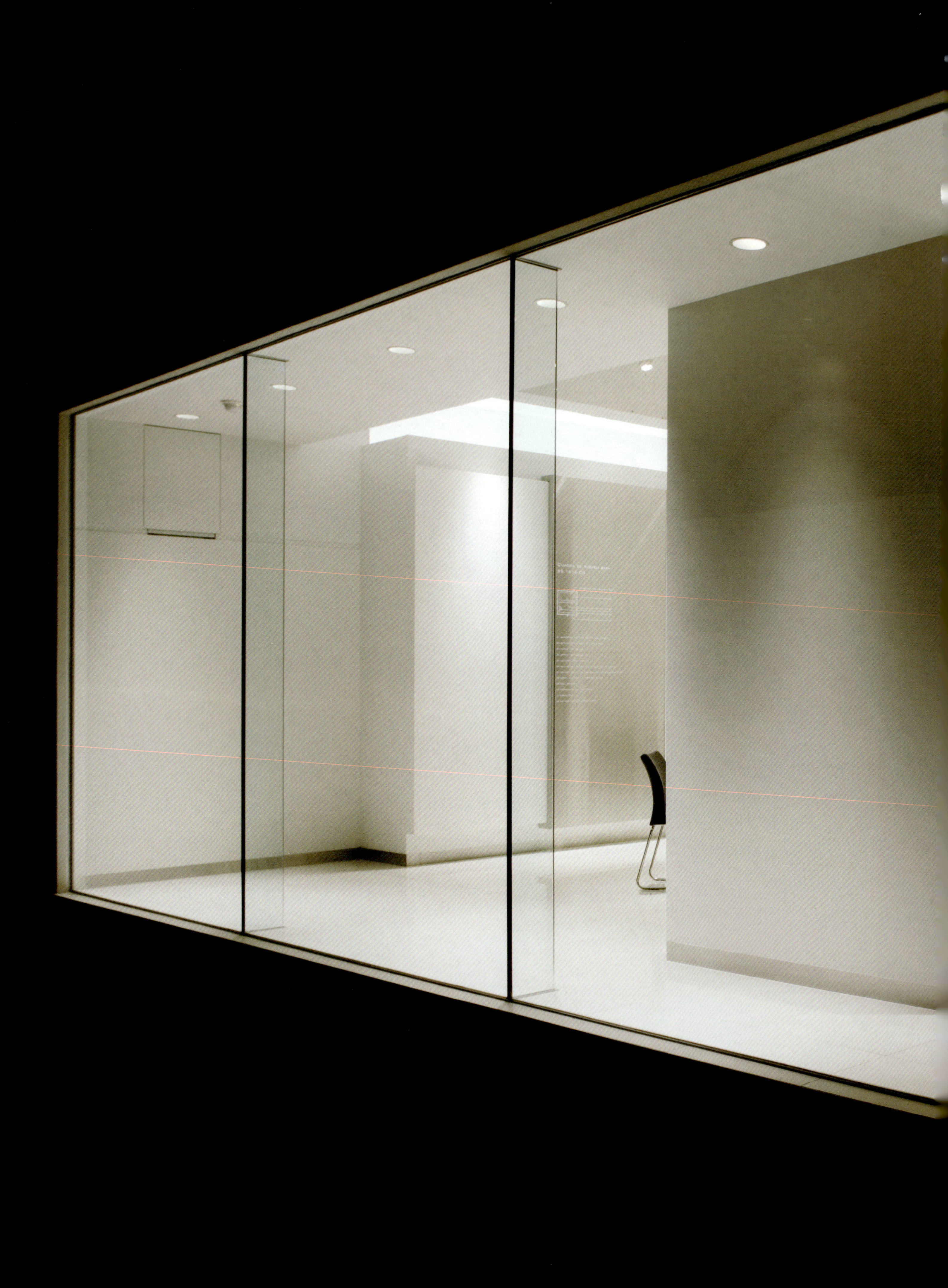

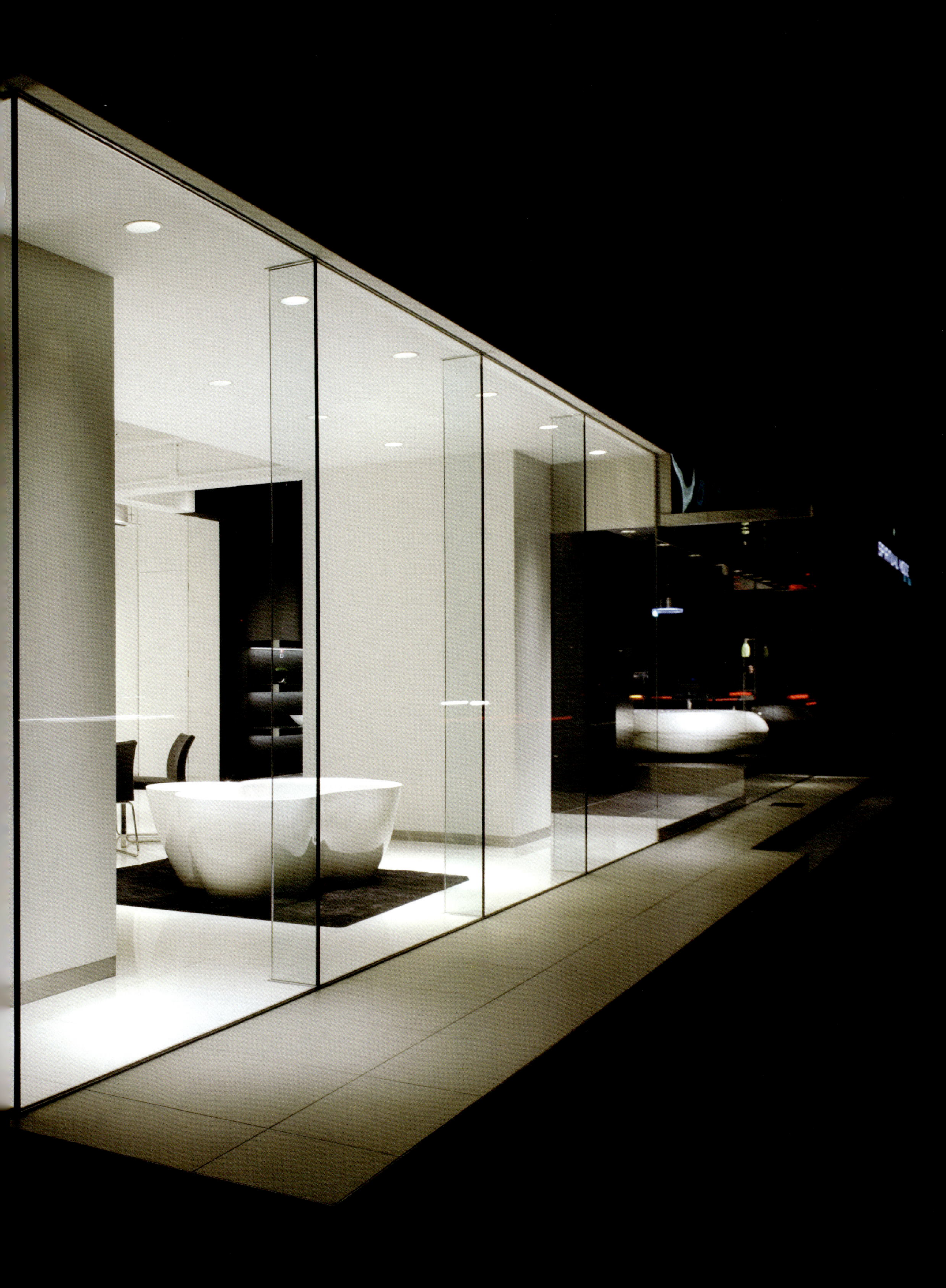

Showroom
SPIRITUAL MODE KYOTO
Kamitoba, Kyoto
スピリチュアルモード　京都
Completion : January 2007
Total area : 201㎡／1F・138㎡　2F・63㎡

P.122・123	外観
P.124・125	外部から接客スペースを見る
P.126 左上	1階フロアから階段室を見る
P.126 右上	手すりのディテール
P.126 左下	洗面台
P.127 上	吹き抜けを見下ろす
P.127 左下	型板ガラスのディテール
P.127 右下	トイレ内
P.122・123	The facade.
P.124・125	The showroom.
P.126 upper left	The stairs to the second floor.
P.126 upper right	The detail of the the stairs handrail.
P.126 lower left	The wash basin.
P.127 upper	A look down at the first floor.
P.127 upper	A look down at the first floor from the second floor.
P.127 lower left	The detail of the forming glass.
P.127 lower right	The rest room.

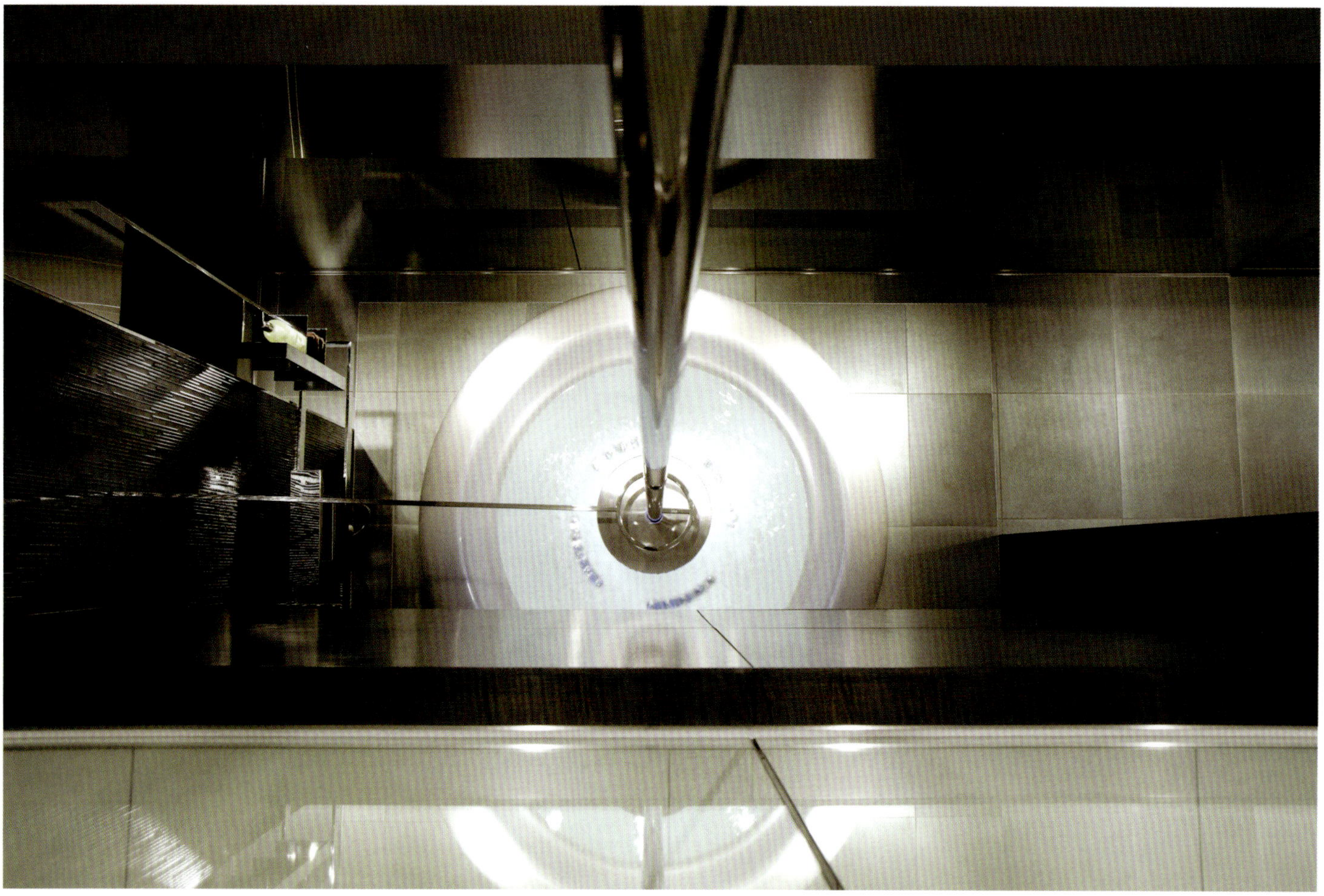

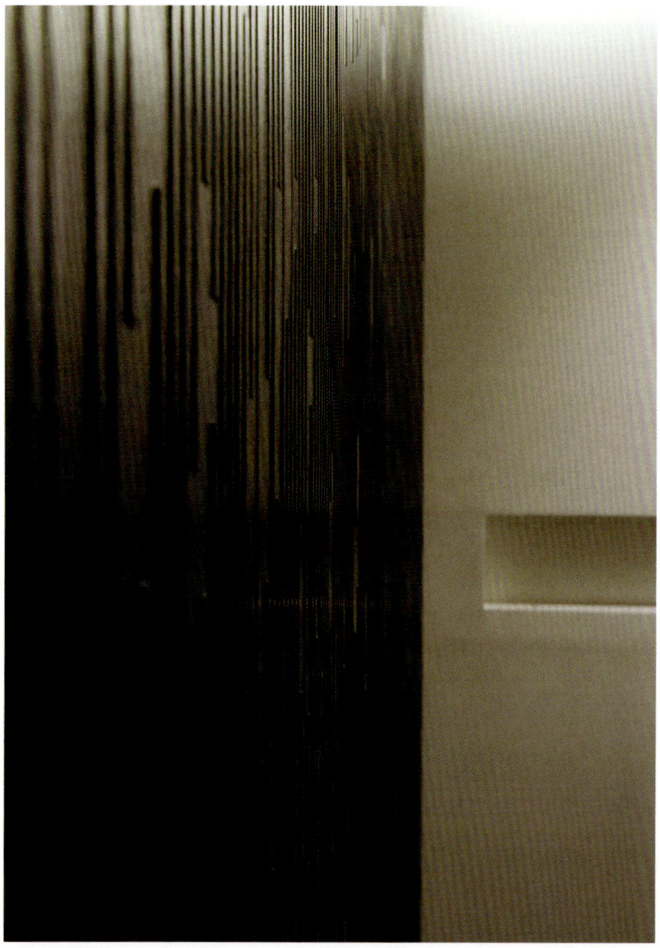

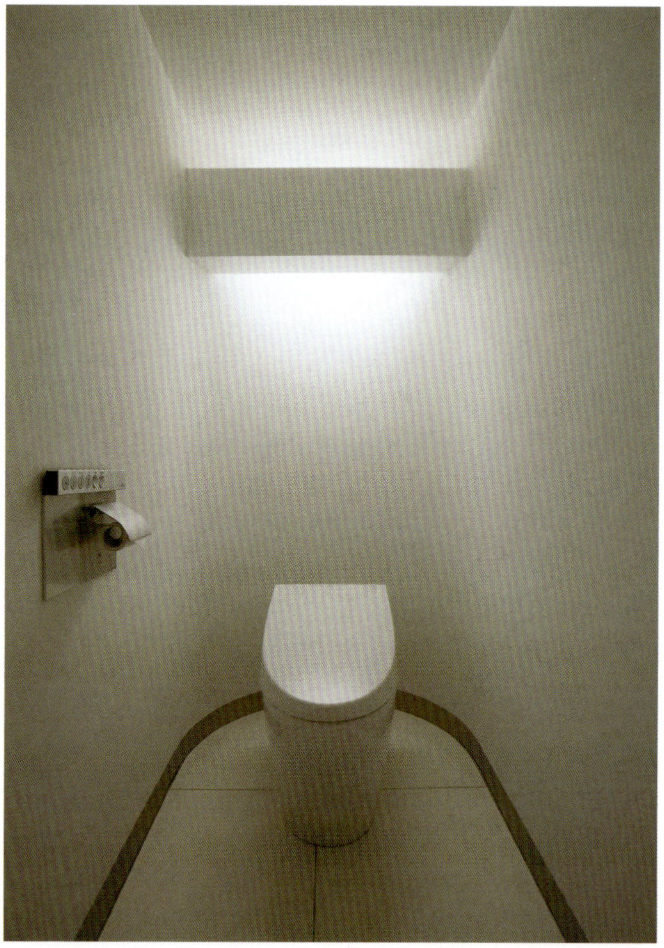

DCMX SITE

Showroom
DCMX SITE
Shinjuku, Tokyo
DCMXサイト
Completion : May 2006
Total area : 320㎡

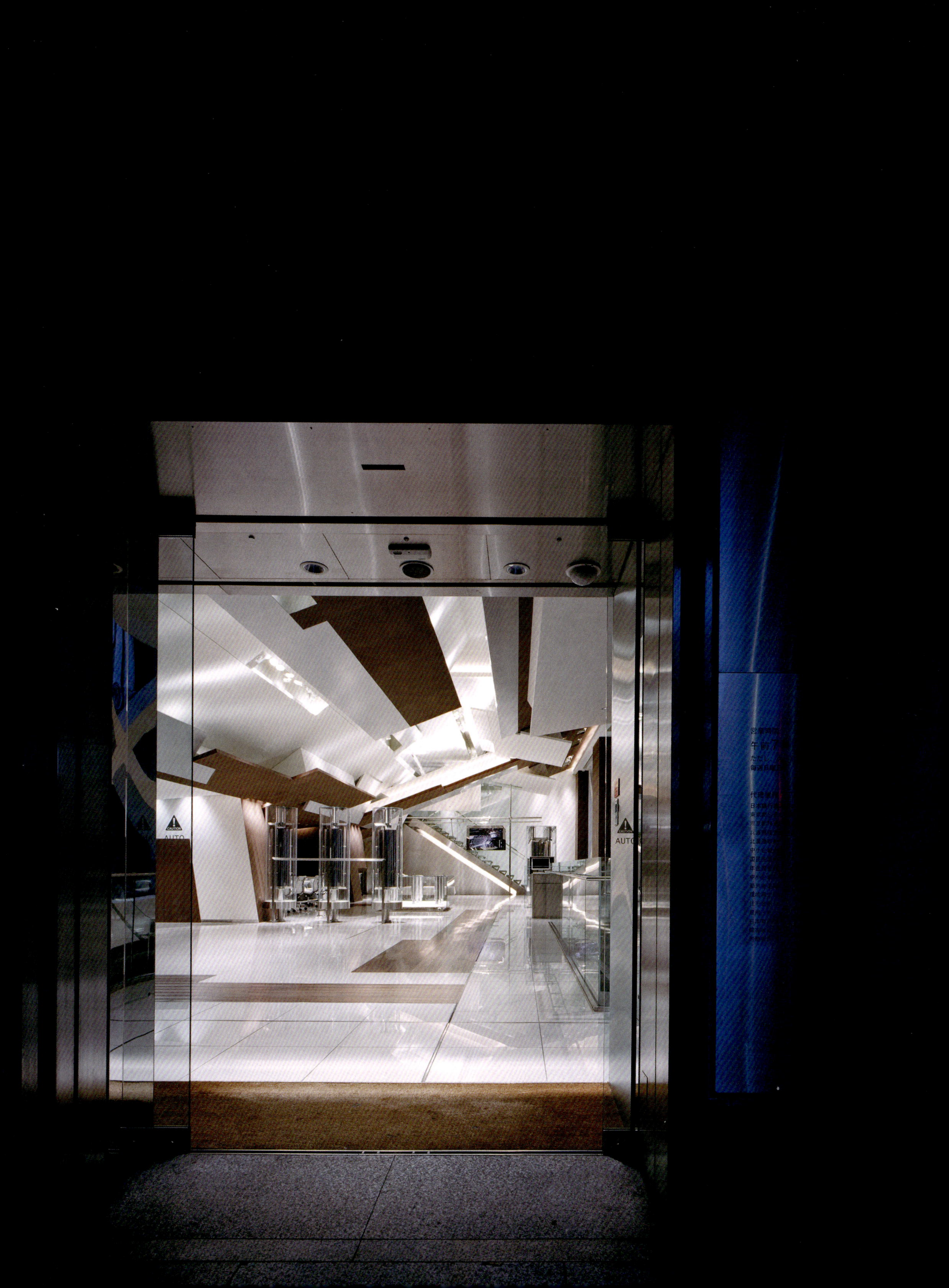
AUTO

130

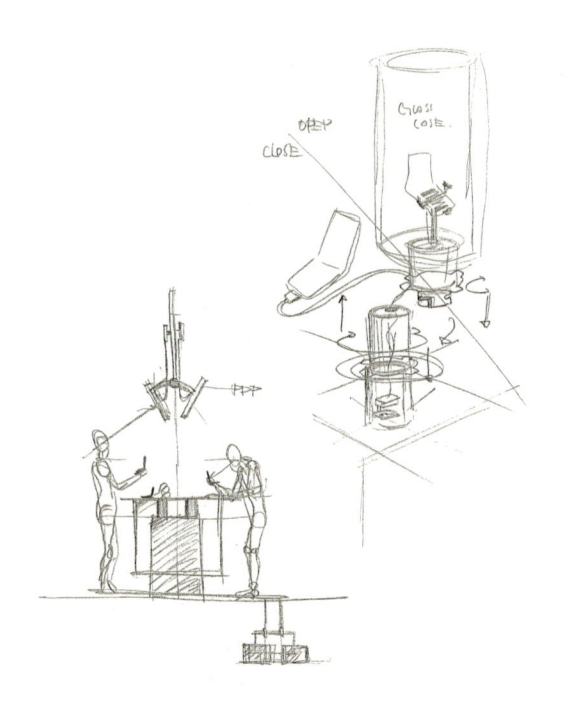

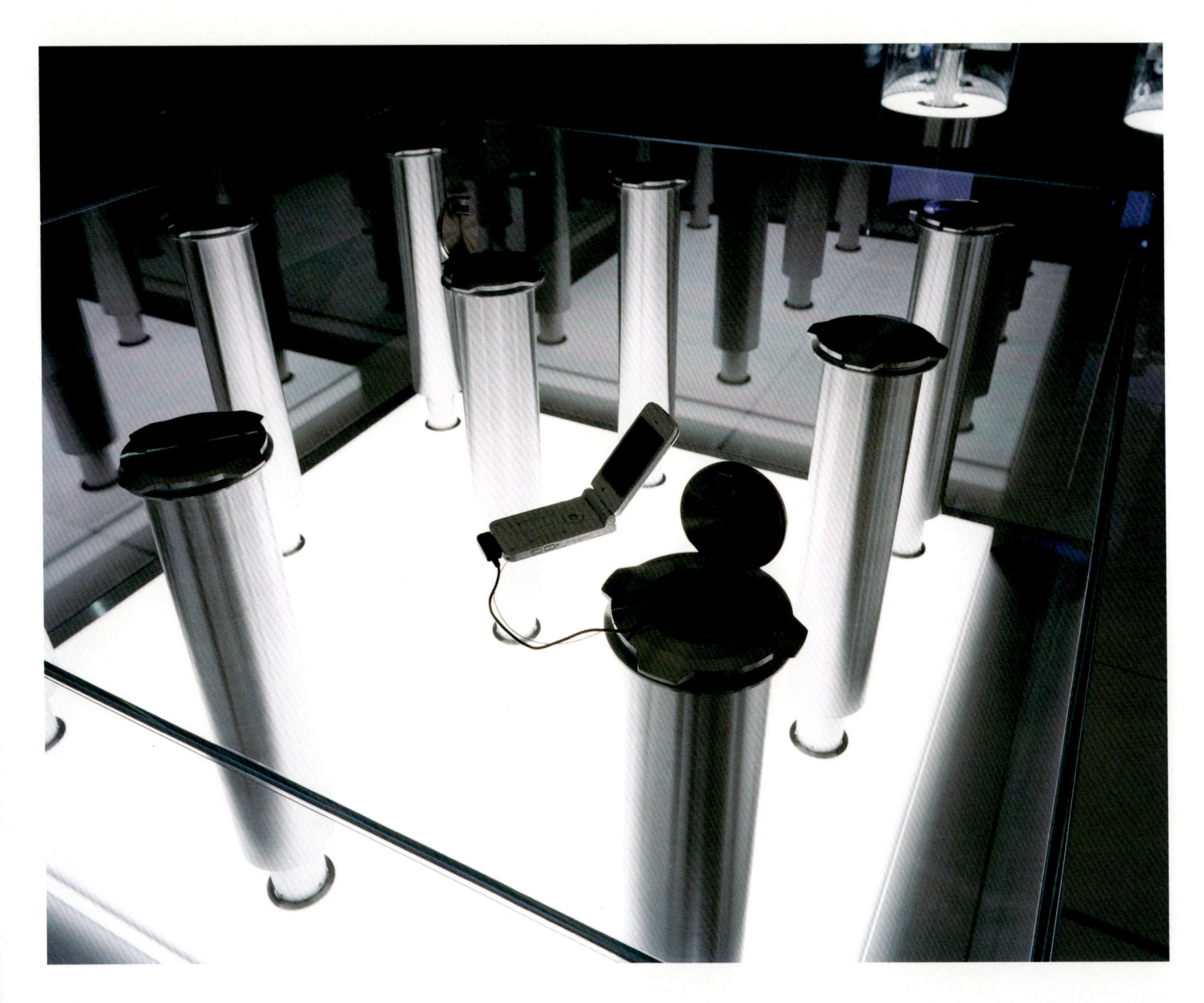

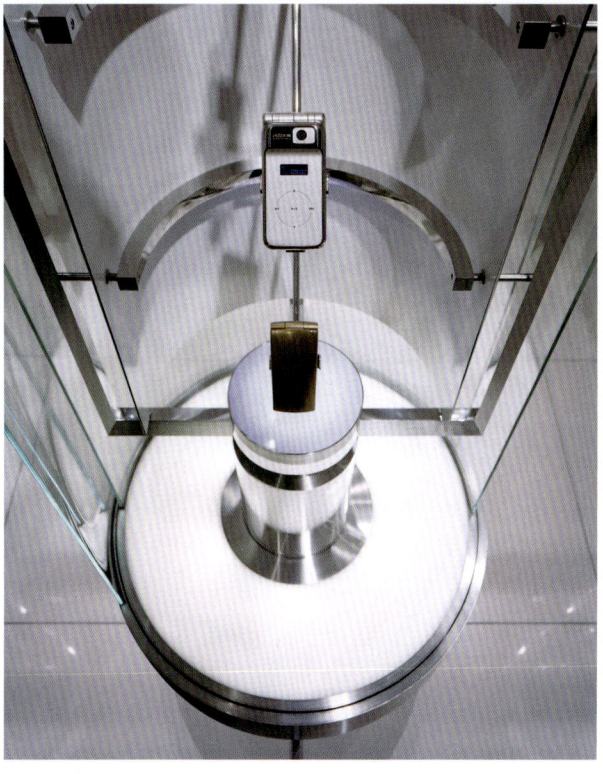

P.128	店内を見返す
P.129	エントランスから店内を見通す。手前左手は銀行ATMコーナー
P.130 上	動態展示什器
P.130 下	動態展示什器ディテール。ステンレス製シリンダーから携帯電話用の充電コードが引き出される
P.131 上	階段ステップのディテール
P.131 下	静態展示什器の扉を開けた状態
P.128	A view of the interior.
P.129	The entrance.
P.130 upper	The display table.
P.130 lower	Detail of the display table.
P.131 upper	Detail of the stairs.
P.131 lower	The detail of the stairs.

Hair Salon
K-TWO UMEDA
Umeda, Osaka
ケイ・ツー 梅田店
Completion : May 1998
Total area : 118㎡

P.132 上　カットコーナーエンドのアール壁面
P.132 下　待合カウンター
P132・133　アプローチ階段を見下ろす
P.132 上　The haircut corner.
P.132 下　The waiting space.
P132・133　The approach stairs.

K-TWO UMEDA

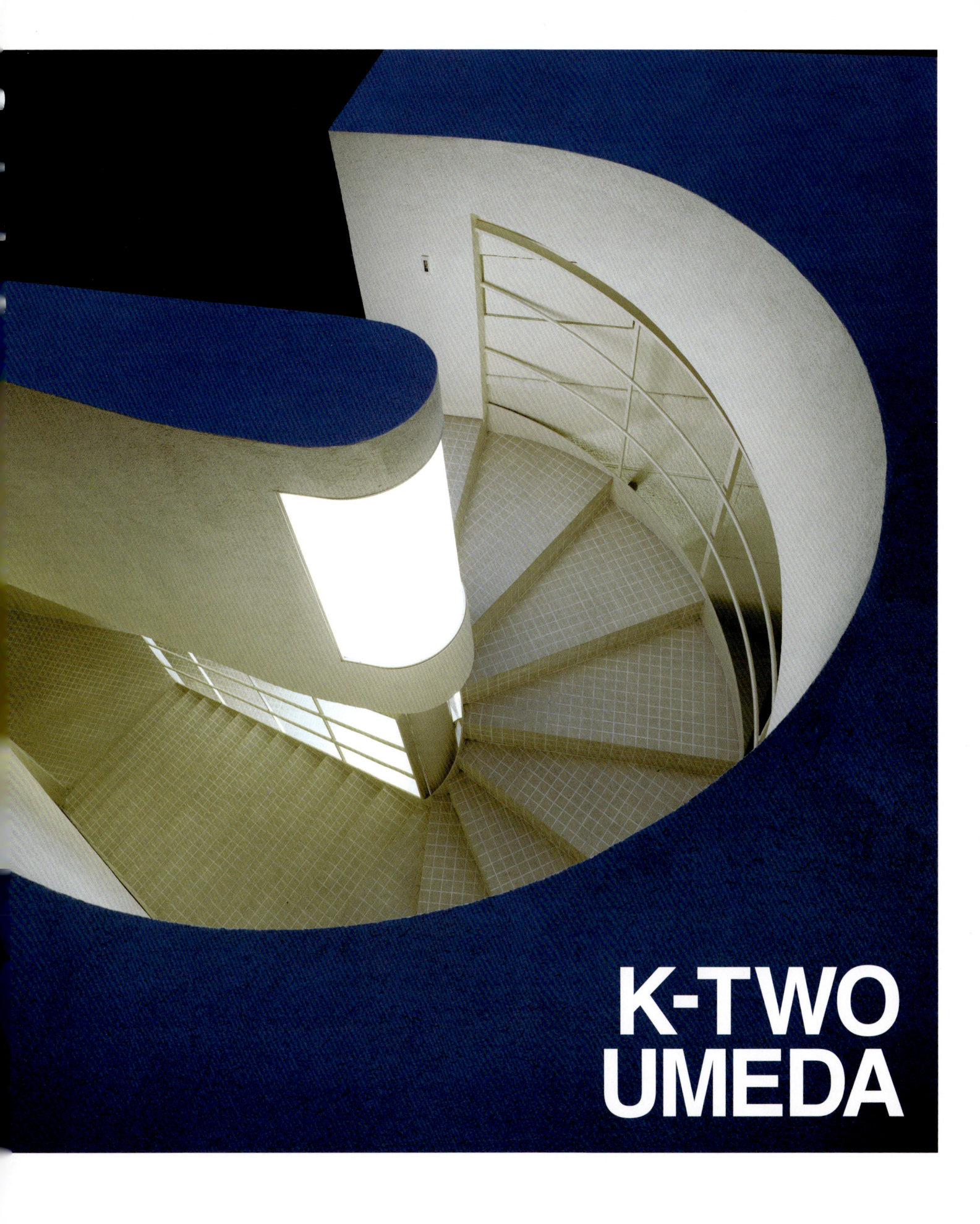

K-TWO
SHINSAIBASHI

Hair Salon
K-TWO SHINSAIBASHI
Shinsaibashi, Osaka
ケイ・ツー　心斎橋店
Completion : September 1999
Total area : 470㎡

P.134・135	ギャラリーを兼ねた待合いスペース
P.136 上	開口部側に並ぶカットシート
P.136 下	外部から天井に120本並ぶ円筒状の照明器具を見る。1本の器具に2本のFLが内蔵
P.137 上	アール型自立パーティション
P.137 下	ガラスで仕切られたメーク&ネイルスペース
P.134・135	The waiting space.
P.136 upper	The haircut space.
P.136 lower	A look up at the interior from outside.
P.137 upper	The curved surface partition.
P.137 lower	The makeup & nail space.

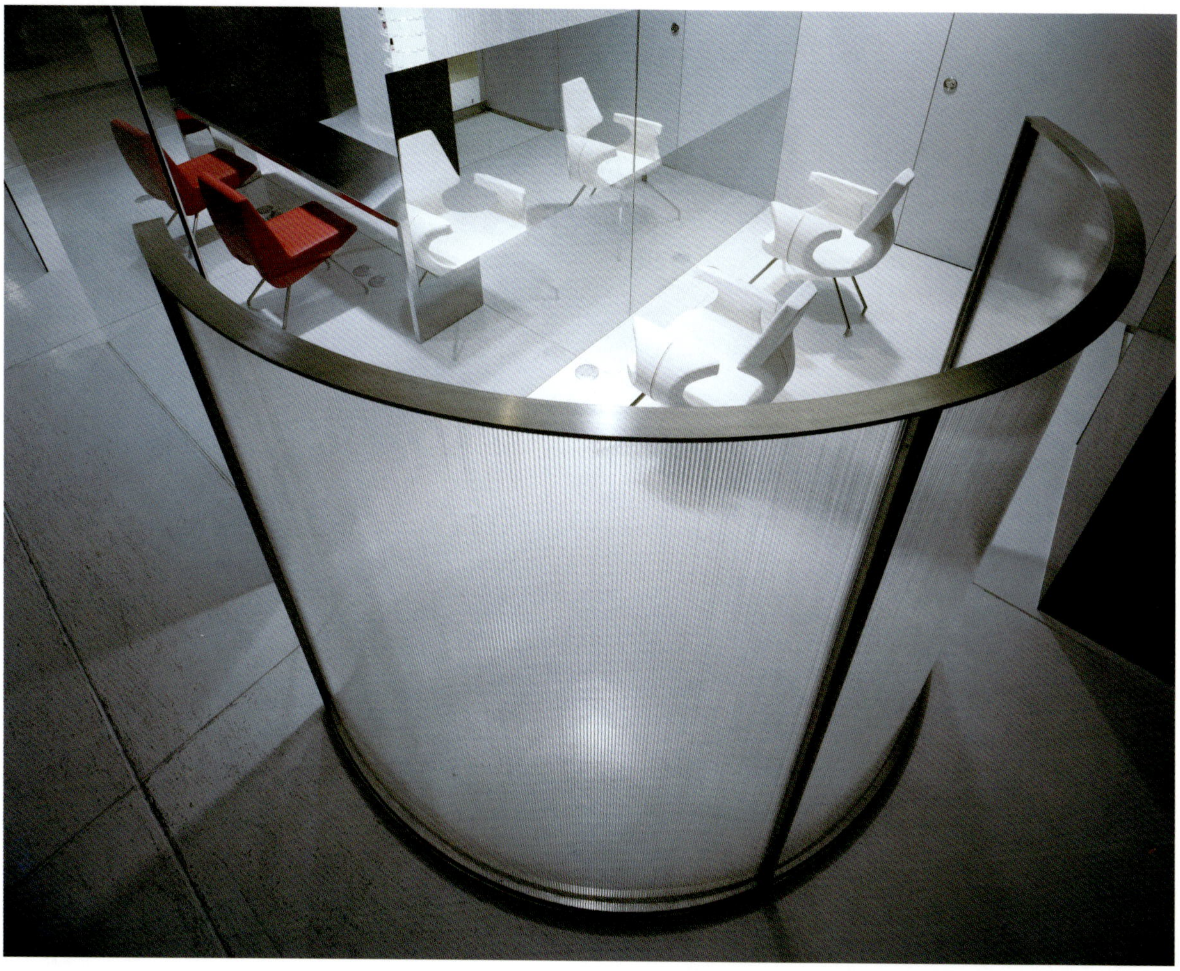

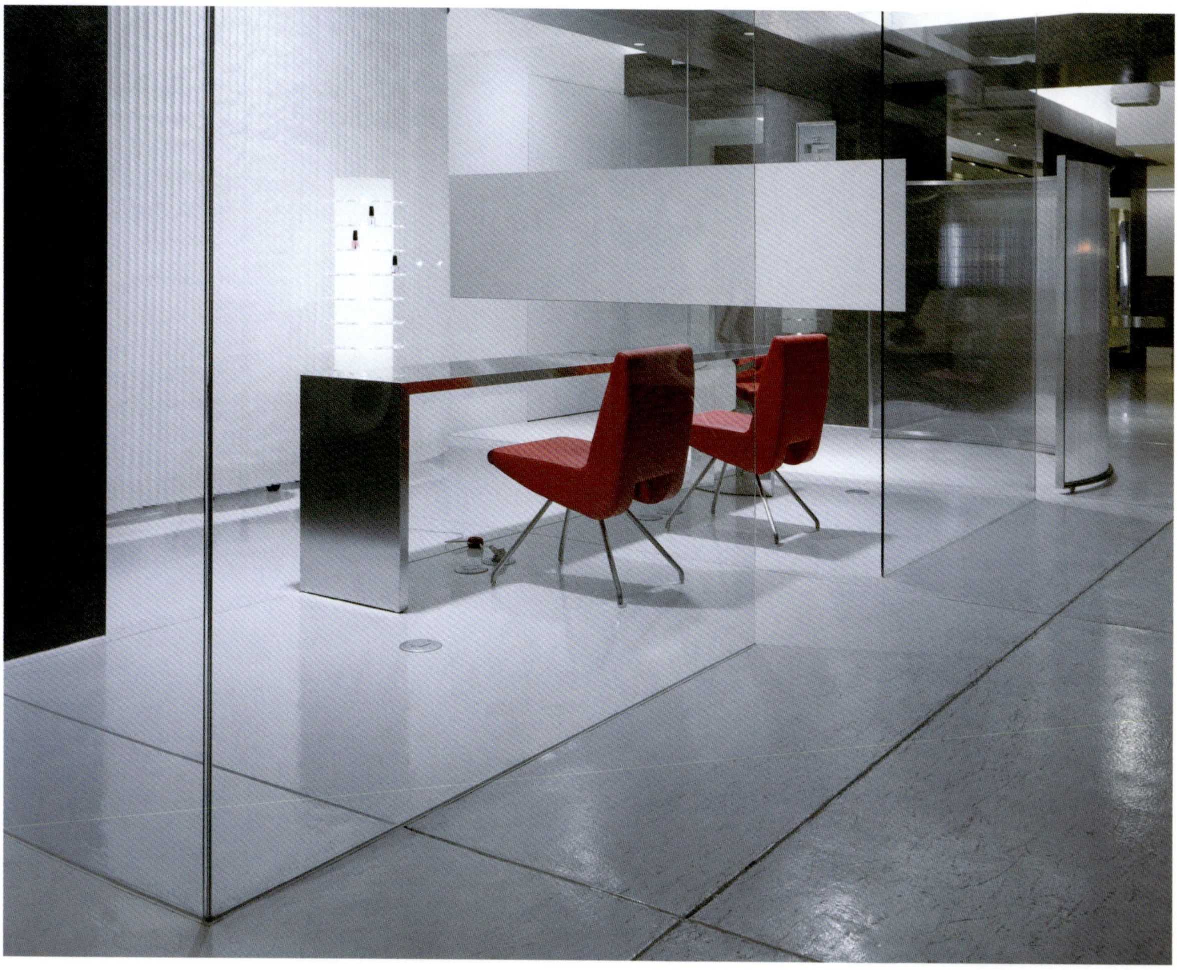

SALON

138

Hair Salon
SALON
Ginza, Tokyo
サロン
Completion : March 2008
Total area : 301㎡

P.138 上	レセプションカウンター。店内導入部はブラウンの色調
P.138 下	スタイリングルーム入り口
P.139 上	スタイリングルーム。全体に白が用いられている
P.139 下	スタイリングルームから入り口を見返す
P.138 upper	The reception counter.
P.138 lower	The entrance of styling room.
P.139 upper・lower	The styling room.

ANAYI

ANAYI SHINJUKU ISETAN

Boutique
ANAYI SHINJUKU ISETAN
Shinjuku, Tokyo
アナイ　新宿伊勢丹店
Completion：August 2004　Total area：74㎡

P.140・141　共用通路から見た店内全景。
　　　　　　木とブロンズ色に着色されたアルミで壁面を構成
P.141　　　柱什器まわり
P.140・141　A view of the entire shop.
P.141　　　Pillar fixture.

ANAYI HIROSHIMA FUKUYA EKIMAE

Boutique
ANAYI HIROSHIMA FUKUYA EKIMAE
Minami-ku, Hiroshima
アナイ　福屋広島駅前店
Completion : February 2005
Total area : 66㎡

P.142 上　　店内を通して見る
P.142 下　　幾何学ラインで構成された壁面
P.143 上　　ディスプレイスペース越しに店内を見る
P.143 下　　共用通路から店内を見る
P.142 upper　A view of the entire shop.
P.142 lower　The wall.
P.143 upper　The display case.
P.143 lower　A view of the shop from outside.

ESSENCE OF ANAYI TOKYO MIDTOWN

Boutique
ESSENCE OF ANAYI TOKYO MIDTOWN
Roppongi, Tokyo
エッセンス オブ アナイ　東京ミッドタウン店
Completion：March 2007
Total area：112㎡

P.144	ジュエリーショーケース越しにレジカウンターと壁面を見る
P.145 上	ショップフロント
P.145 左下	壁面什器
P.145 右下	棚什器
P.144	A view of the checkout counter.
P.145 upper	The facade.
P.145 lower left	The display wall.
P.145 lower right	The display shelf.

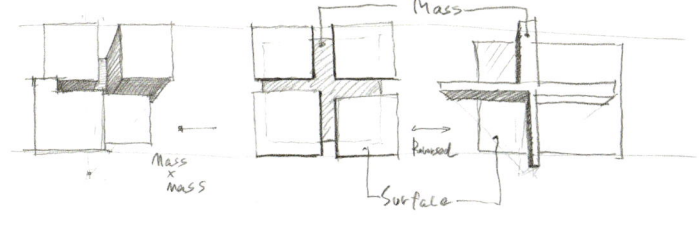

Boutique
ANAYI NISHINOMIYA HANKYU
Nishinomiya, Hyogo
アナイ　西宮阪急店
Completion : November
Total area : 83㎡

P.146 上　　　　　店内を見通す
P.146 下・P.147　造作壁を見る
P.146 upper　　　A view of the shop.
P.146 lower・P.147　Detail of the wall.

ANAYI NISHINOMIYA HANKYU

MANOUQUA

SHIN-MARUNOUCHI BUILDING

Boutique
MANOUQUA SHIN-MARUNOUCHI BUILDING
Marunouchi, Tokyo
マヌーカ　新丸ビル店
Completion : August 2007　Total area : 68㎡

P.148　エントランスから店内を見る
P.149　棚什器越しにサークルパターンを
　　　　打ち抜いた壁面を見る
P.148　The entrance.
P.149　The wall in the interior.

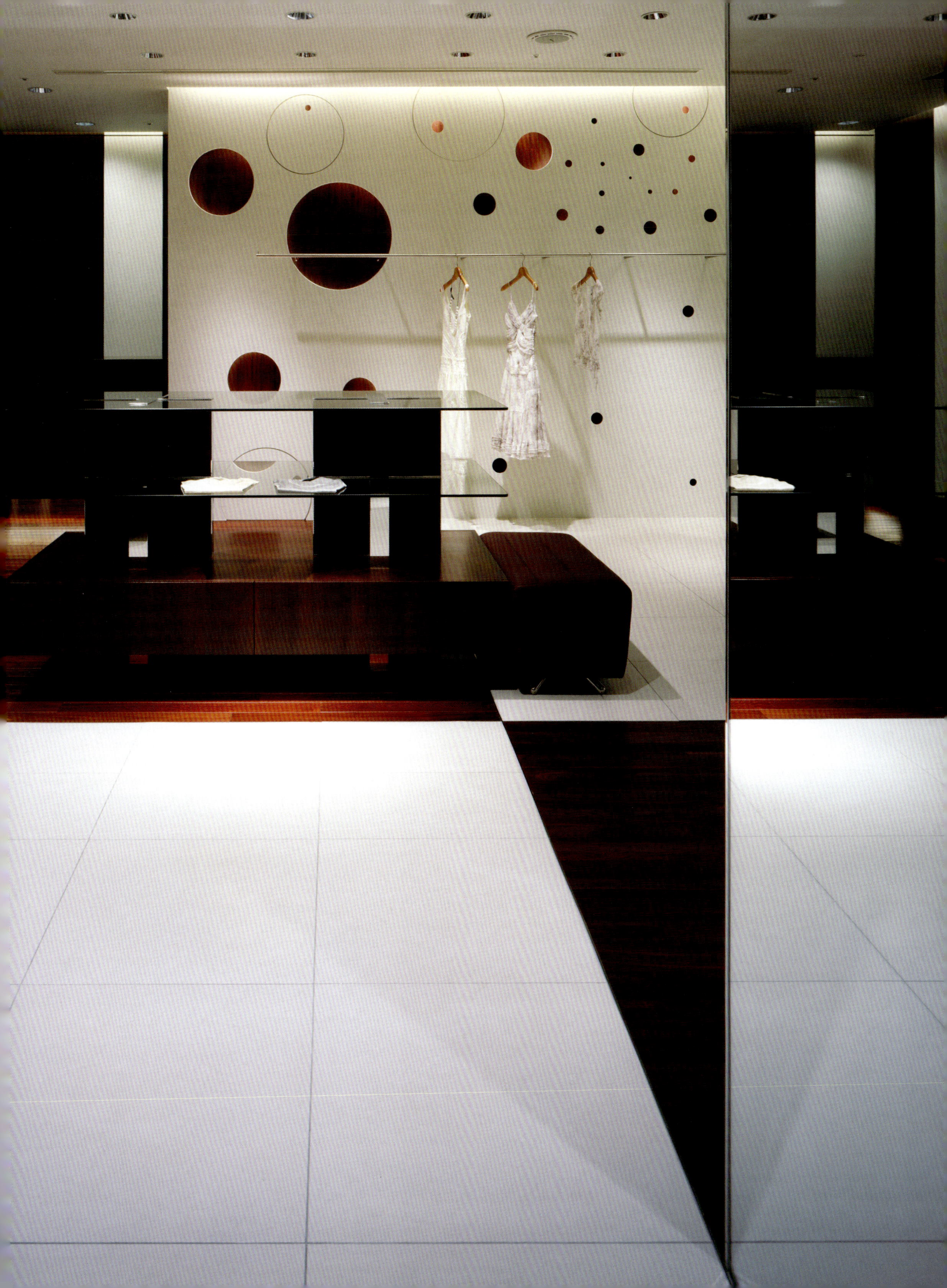

Lifestyle Shop
IXC COLLECTA TAMAGAWA TAKASHIMAYA
Futakotamagawa, Tokyo
イクシー コレクタ　玉川髙島屋店
Completion : September 2003
Total area : 30㎡

店内の壁面を見る。着脱可能な棚やハンガーラックなどが取り付けられている
The wall of the shop.

IXC COLLECTA TAMAGAWA TAKASHIMAYA

INHALE+ EXHALE KOBE FASHION MART

Boutique
INHALE+EXHALE KOBE FASHION MART
Higashinada-ku, Kobe
インヘイル＋エクスヘイル　神戸ファッションマート店
Completion : September 1996　Total area : 162㎡

P.152・153　ファサード
P.152・153　The facade.

INHALE+ EXHALE SHINKOBE ORIENTAL HOTEL

Boutique
INHALE+EXHALE SHINKOBE ORIENTAL HOTEL
Chuo-ku, Kobe
インヘイル+エクスヘイル　新神戸オリエンタルホテル店
Completion：April 1998　Total area：147㎡

P.154　　　　店内からエントランス方向を見る
P.155 上　　オリジナルのハンガーラックが置かれたレジカウンター前
P.155 下　　ファサード
P.154　　　　The display space.
P.155 upper　Ditto.
P.155 lower　The facade.

INTERVIEW 3

Q. どういうものからデザインをインスパイアされますか。

文田 興味を持って何かを探すという行為自体、もはや日常化してしまっていて、これというものがないのですが、素材などに関しては常に気にしていますね。また、「見慣れたものを見慣れないものにする」という行為については、よく考えています。どういうことかと言うと、以前、お皿を沢山重ね、物販店のディスプレイ台にしたことがありますが、そういった「日常の要素を別方向から見る」ような行為のことです。突き詰めていくと、「まだ顕在化していないものを顕在化させる」ことが理想です。

人は基本的に、「入って」「触って」「使う」ことで空間を認識します。しかし、例えば詩のように、言葉一つひとつでは伝えられないけれど、いくつかの言葉を組み合わせることで意味を持ち、誰しもが持っている「言葉にならない感覚」を、私は空間や形に表現するようなことをしたいと思っています。それは、「目で見る」「耳で聞く」「舌で味わう」こととは違って、普段意識しないような部分をぐっと引っ張り出してきて、形にして、いつの間にか言葉になっている、といったような感覚です。

昔読んだ建築の本にあった、「中心の喪失」という言葉がとても印象に残っています。それは、当時、私の頭の中にあったもやもやしたものを整理するのにぴったりの言葉でした。いろいろなものが集まっていて、それぞれが主張し過ぎることでそれぞれが希薄になるような相関関係の時代、感覚を言い表してくれていたのだと思います。そういう無意識の感覚を共鳴させるようなことを、形を扱う者として空間で実現すべきだと考えています。

それを見た人が「そう、こんな気持ちあったよなあ」と感じてもらえる空間です。

20代前半の頃まで「感性」という言葉が嫌いでした。当時、何かにつけて感性という言葉が用いられていましたが、感性という言葉ほど曖昧で根拠のないものはないと思っていました。同時に、そもそもデザインの存在が不安定なものだと思っていて、感性より理論的な根拠が欲しいと感じ、例えば、自分なりの方程式があって、そこに与件をはめ込めば答えが出るようなものがあれば、悩まなくて済むと考えていたんです。その方程式はとても高次元なもので、まだ解明できていないだけかもしれませんが、今では、未だ顕在化されていないものを顕在化するという行為は、方程式だけで導かれるものではなく、研ぎすまされた感覚こそ必要なのかもしれないとも感じています。

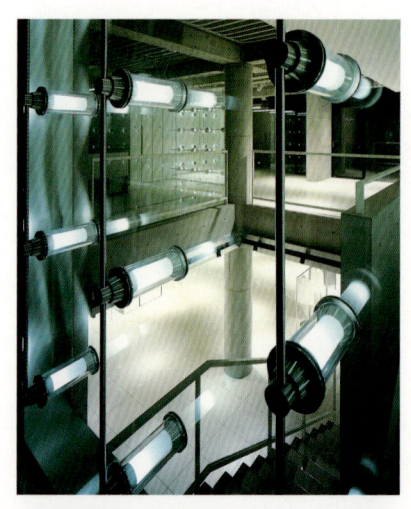

DESIGN PHILOSOPHY
デザイン・フィロソフィー

Q.好きなもの、こだわりのあるものは何かありますか。

文田 好きなもの……う〜ん。私はいろいろな"部分"というか、ディテールが好きですね。例えば、飛行機のボディーから出てくるゴツい車輪や周辺の複雑な機構、開閉ハッチなどのディテール、クルマで言うとランボルギーニなんかの形が好きです。ランボルギーニは、究極的なスピードを追求した結果生まれたフォルムが、まるで戦闘機のような形状として採り入れられている。ある種、究極的な目的の末、生まれてきた究極的な存在やディテールにはやはり惹かれるものがあります。

ただここで興味深いのは、究極の機能性を追求すれば、カタチはすべて最終的に同じ解答になっていくはずなのに、そうはなっていない。つまり、極端な例として戦闘機などのカタチが、国や時代、文化によっても異なっているのが面白いと感じます。それは前述した、時代性やその時々の科学技術力、人の感性といったものが作用しておのおのに独創性が備わっているからだと思います。

そういった究極の存在、ディテールを表現したくなるのは常ですが、デザインという行為には「我慢」が大切と考え、ネガティブな意味ではなく、抑えている部分もあります。それは、他者の仕事、あるいは車のデザインを見て、「抑え」のあるデザインに気品を感じることがあるからです。ディテールは、大きく二つに分けられます。一つは、「見せる、表現するためのディテール」「構造やシステムを明らかにするためのディテール」といった技術力の表現と言えるもの。もう一つは、消すためのディテール、「ディテールレスのためのディテール」です。例えば、ブティックの扉で「どのように蝶番を隠そうか」あるいは、「扉ではなく開閉するパネルとして考えれば、どう在るべきか」というときに考える部分です。

来店するお客さんからすれば、蝶番が付いていようが付いていまいがどちらでもよいのですが、空間はそういった一つひとつのディテールが積み上がって、全体のクオリティーが決まっていくと思っています。そこでは、「神は細部に宿る」というミース・ファン・デル・ローエの言葉の支えもあって、常に「もっと良い方法はないか」と突き詰めながらデザインしています。

〈聞き手 高橋正明〉

> 言葉一つひとつでは伝えられないけれど、
> いくつかの言葉を組み合わせることで意味を持ち、
> 誰しもが持っている「言葉にならない感覚」を、
> 私は空間や形に表現するようなことをしたい

FUMITA
DESIGNOFFICE

Office
FUMITA DESIGN OFFICE
Daikanyama, Tokyo
文田昭仁デザインオフィス
Completion : December 2007   Total area : 232㎡

The act of looking for something I'm interested in has already become commonplace for me, and often there's no one particular thing I'm looking for, but I am always paying attention to material. Also, "making something people are used to seeing look unfamiliar" is something I often think about.

興味を持って何かを探すという行為自体、もはや日常化してしまっていて、これというものがないのですが、
素材などに関しては常に気にしていますね。また、「見慣れたものを見慣れないものにする」という行為については、よく考えています。

P.158　　　　天井を間接照明で照らすスタッフルーム
P.159 左　　 大理石貼りの壁面
P.159 右　　 隠し扉の奥に打ち合わせソファコーナー
P.158　　　　The staff room.
P.159 left　　The wall of marble.
P.159 right　 The camouflage meeting room.

P.152 上　　　エントランス
P.152 下　　　ミーティングルームからエントランス方向を見返す
P.152 upper　The entrance.
P.152 lower　The entrance from the meeting room.

P.153 上　　　ミーティングルーム
P.153 下　　　白で統一されたソファコーナー
P.153 upper　The meeting room.
P.153 lower　The sofa corner.

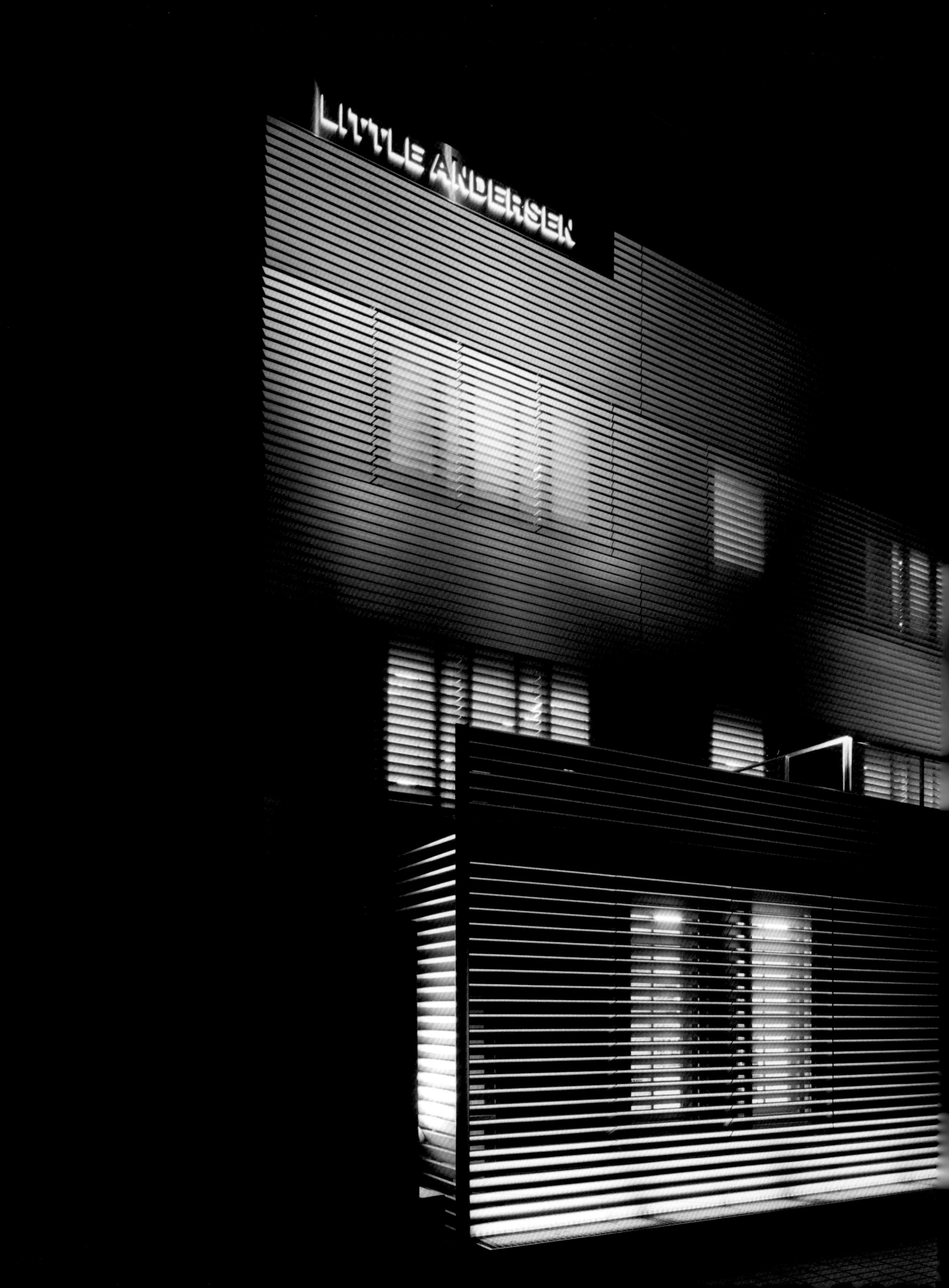
LITTLE ANDERSEN

LITTLE ANDERSEN

Office Exterior
LITTLE ANDERSEN
Shibuya, Tokyo
リトルアンデルセン
Completion : February 2001

P.162・163 水平ルーバーで囲われた外観
P.162・163 The exterior at night.

H-HOUSE

House
H-HOUSE
Shibuya, Tokyo
H邸
Completion：July 2004
Total area：193㎡／B1F・75㎡
1F・72㎡　2F・45㎡

P.164・165　ファサード
P.165　　　スリット状に開口部を設けた建物側面
P.164・165　The facade.
P.165　　　The exterior.

P.160 上　　　　スロープ状の地下駐車場
P.160 下　　　　地階から続く螺旋階段
P.161　　　　　螺旋階段見上げ
P.161 upper　　The underground parking.
P.161 lower　　The spiral staircase.
P.162　　　　　A look up at the spiral staircase.

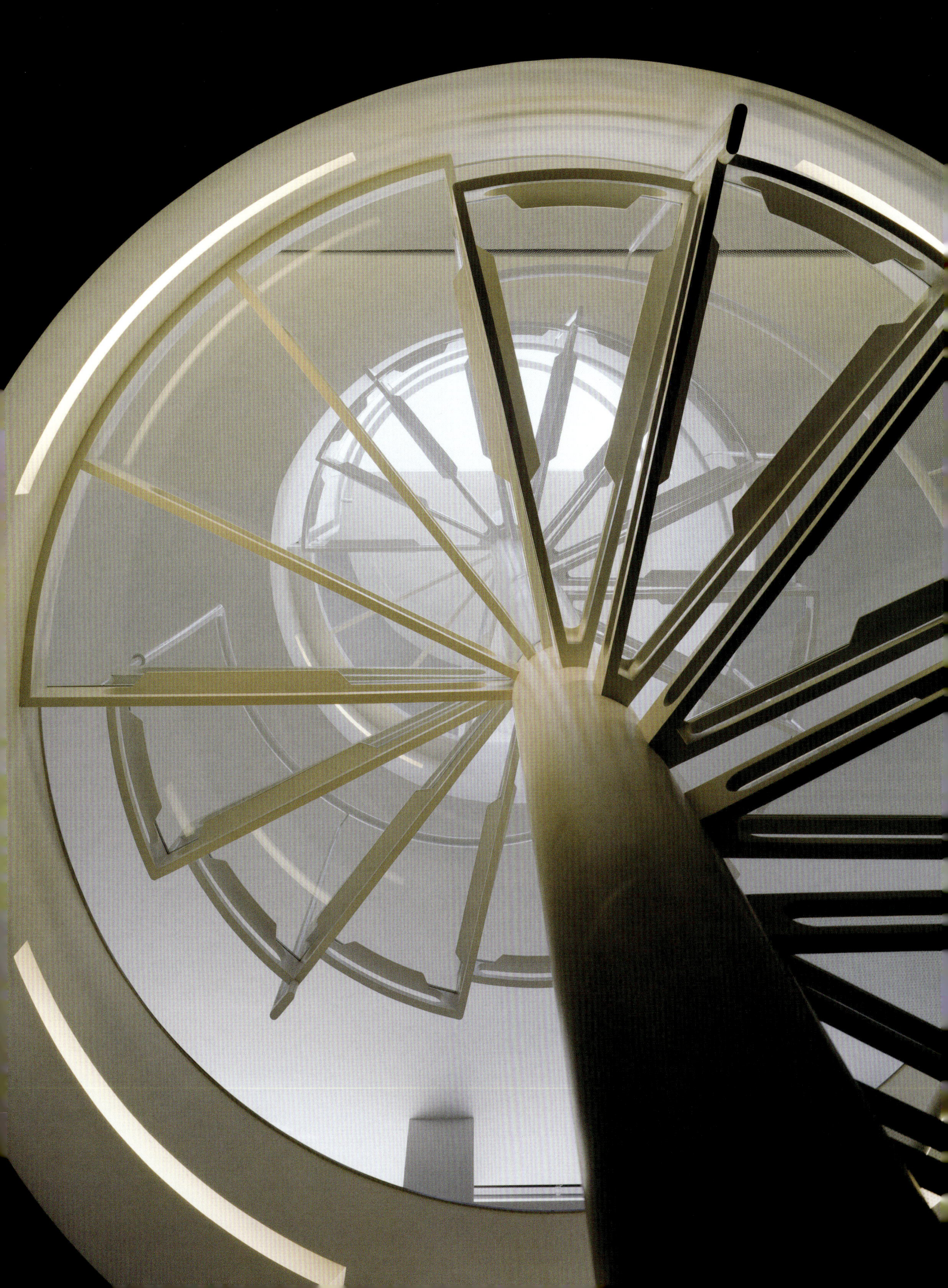

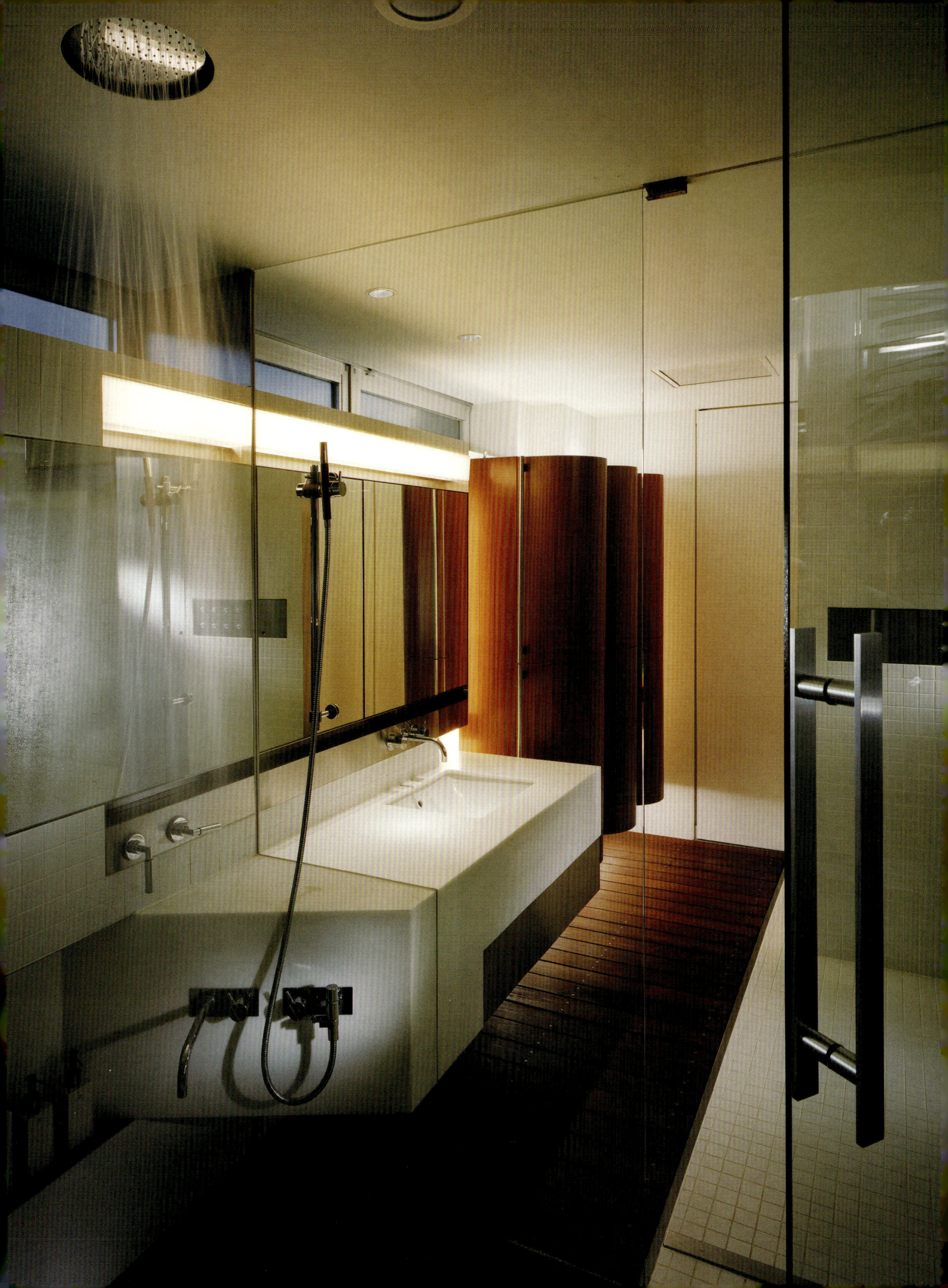

P.162　　　　　　　レインシャワーヘッドを埋め込んだバスルームから洗面所を見る
P.163 上　　　　　寝室、ベッド側から入り口方向を見返す
P.163 下　　　　　ベッドまわり
P.162　　　　　　　The bathroom.
P.163 upper・lower The bed room.

PRODUCT

Exhibition
Tokyo Designers Block 2001
東京デザイナーズブロック2001

2001年のデザインイベントで発表されたインスタレーション。2種の「セミ・ファニチャー」が展示された。一つ目は、チューブ形のエアクッションで照明を包み込み、クッションや照明としての機能を重複させたもの。二つ目は、70年代の日本でよく見られた「ファンシーケース」という洋服カバーをモチーフにした、吊り下げ式クローゼット。どちらも家具として機能しながら、存在感は曖昧な「家具未満」のものとしてつくられた。

This is an installation art project announced at a 2001 design event. Two types of "semi furniture" were on display. The first consisted of lights wrapped in tubular air cushions, which served the functions of both cushions and lights. The second was a hanging closet with a motif of the "fancy case" clothing covers often seen in the Japan of the 1970s. Both types were designed to be "less than furniture," having the function of furniture but an ambiguous presence.

Tokyo Designers Block 2001
Aoyama, Tokyo
Completion : October 2001

Exhibition
Tokyo Designers Block 2003
東京デザイナーズブロック2003

ソファ「：(コロン)」は、相似形の揺り椅子とオットマンで構成され、座る人の姿勢、重さによって座面の角度が変化する。ランプスタンド「／(スラッシュ)」は、ランプの支柱に通電レールを用い、配線をなくしている。またランプは上下にスライドでき、様々なシーンに対応する。

The sofa ": (colon)" is made up of a rocking chair and ottoman of similar figures and its seat changes angle depending on the posture and weight of the person seated. The light stand "/(slash)" uses an electricity-conducting rail for the lamp's support. eliminating wiring. The lamp can slide up or down to fit a variety of scenes.

1. ソファ「：(コロン)」
2. 照明スタンド「／(スラッシュ)」
1. The sofa ": (colon)"
2. The illuminator "/ (slash)"

Tokyo Designers Block 2003
Aoyama, Tokyo
Completion : October 2003

Bathtub
BEIGNET
ベニエ

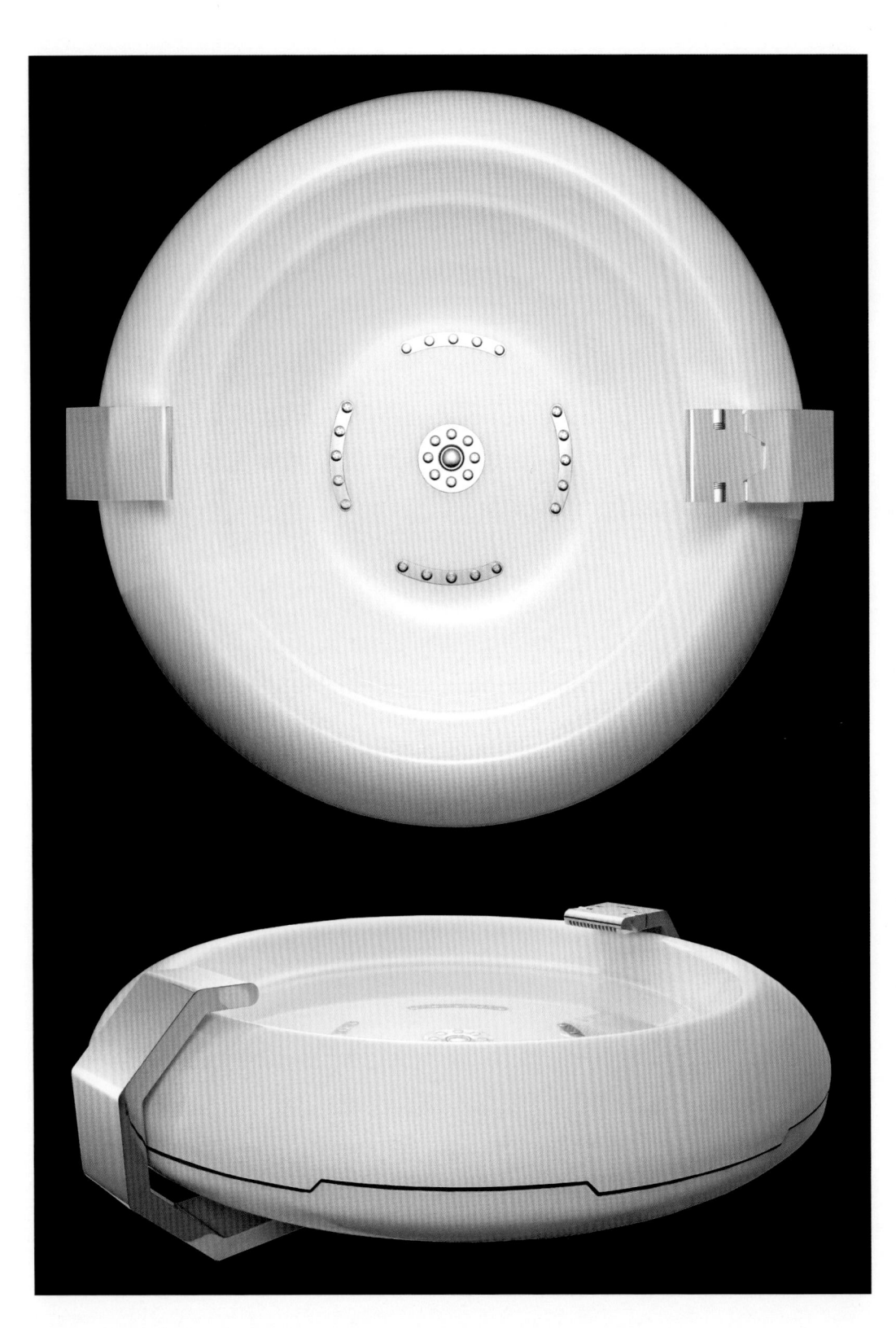

「スピリチュアルモード 南青山店」の設計と同時にデザインされた。シンプルな円形とし、アクリル製の浴槽に、SUSを用いた水栓まわりなど、シンメトリーなフォルムにつくり上げられている。水栓のダイヤルは、引き出して回す際の重みに粘りのある感じを持たせるようデザインされ。使用者が使用感や充実感を味わえるよう考えられた。

This bathtub was designed at the same time as the Spiritual Mode Minami Aoyama store. With a simple circular shape, the acrylic bathtub was given a symmetrical form, including the stainless-steel faucet. The faucet dial was designed so that the user would feel viscosity in the resistance encountered when pulling out and turning it. It was intended to give the user a sense of utility and completeness.

BEIGNET
2005年発表
Size：W2000×D2000×H540
Brand Name：SPIRITUAL MODE

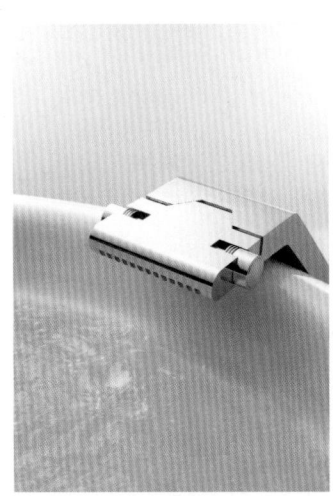

Accessory
EMF Collection
EMFコレクション

アクセサリー、ジュエリーの価値観でデザインしないことで生まれる美しい造形が試みられた。ステンレススチールの二つの素材的特徴を高めるよう考えられており、一つ目は、金属の持つ重量感。二つ目は、極薄のメッシュ状とし、重ねることでる表情の変化を生み、金属の不透明感、半透明感が表現されている。

Fumita tried to create something beautiful by not designing these accessories based on the values of accessories and jewelry. He wanted to elevate two characteristics of stainless steel. For the first, it was the weight of metal. For the second, he made a ultrathin mesh and through changes brought about by piling up layers of mesh, he expresses the opacity and semitransparency of metal.

EMF Collection
2007年発表
Brand Name：ete ＋

Vase	Vase
nest	**face**
ネスト	フェイス

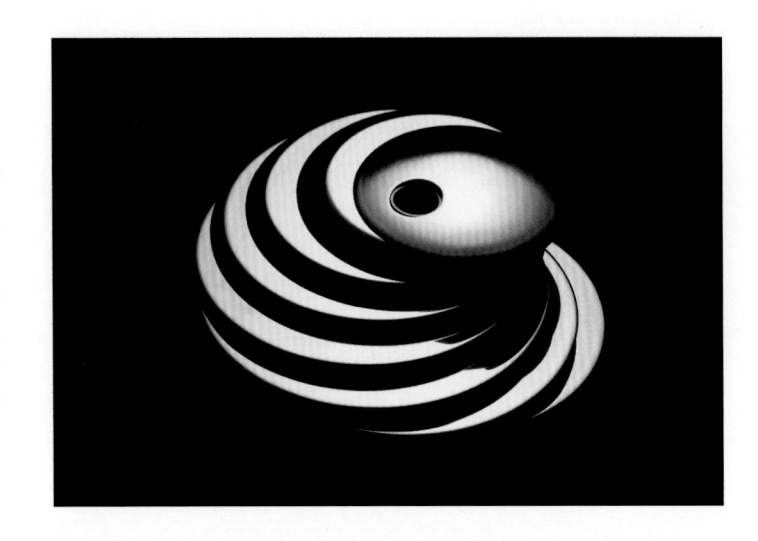

nest
2008年発表
Brand Name：YOnoBI

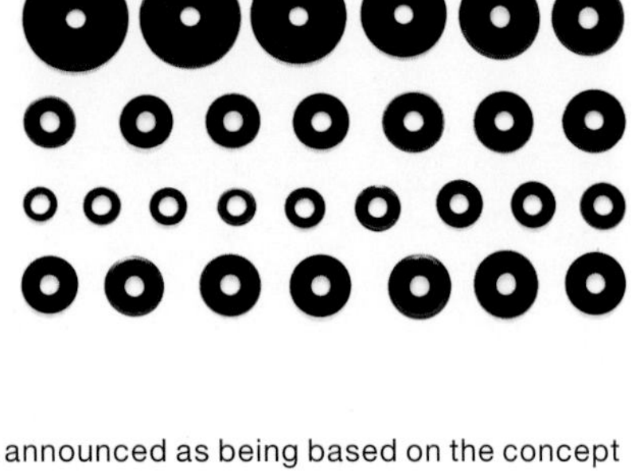

face
2008年発表
Brand Name：YOnoBI

YOnoBIのプロジェクトとして、日本の伝統工芸とコンテンポラリーデザインのコラボレーションというコンセプトで発表されたプロダクト。「ネスト」と「フェイス」は、一輪差しの花器。複数枚重ねたプレートをスライドさせることで、フォルムを自在に変えられる。生ける花の形、ボリュームに花器を合わせることができる。

This project of the YOnoBI was announced as being based on the concept of a collaboration between traditional Japanese industrial arts and contemporary design.
"Nest" and "face" are single-flower vases. Their forms can be freely changed by sliding several layers of piled up plates. The vases can be changed to suit the shape and size of the flower.

Aroma Pot
pebble
ペブル

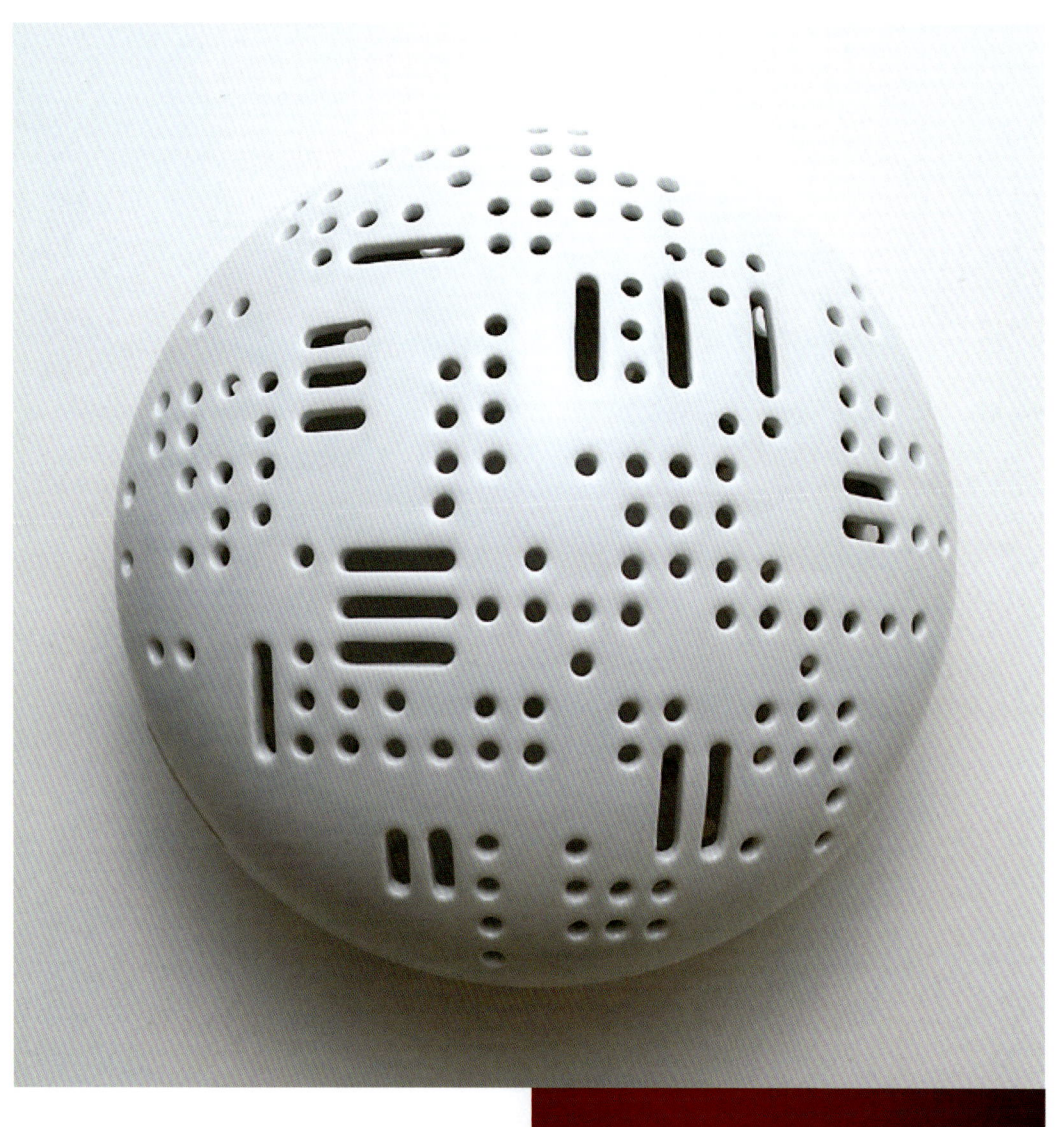

YOnoBIのプロジェクトとして、つくられた波佐見焼の磁器製アロマポット。餅のような形をしており、表面には幾何学模様の穴が並ぶ。その穴からは、使用時にアロマの香りとキャンドルの光がこぼれるようつくられ、機能性と美しさがデザインされている。

This is a Hasami-yaki style porcelain aroma pot created as a YOnoBI project. It is shaped like a mochi rice cake and its surface is lined with holes that form a geometric pattern. It was made so that when it is in use, the aroma and candle light overflow through the holes, and it was designed to combine functionality with beauty.

pebble
2005年発表
Brand Name : YOnoBI

DETAIL DESCRIPTION

NISSAN GALLERY GLOBAL HEADQUARTERS

P6
Showroom
NISSAN GALLERY GLOBAL HEADQUARTERS
Minatomirai, Yokohama
日産グローバル本社ギャラリー

P22
Showroom
NISSAN GALLERY GINZA
Ginza, Tokyo
日産銀座ギャラリー

P36
Showroom
NISSAN GALLERY HEADQUARTERS (old)
Ginza, Tokyo
日産本社ギャラリー（旧本社）

P42
Showroom
NISSAN GALLERY SAPPORO
Sapporo, Hokkaido
日産札幌ギャラリー

「日産グローバル本社ギャラリー」は、2009年、東京・銀座より横浜・みなとみらいに移転した本社に付帯するショールームとして計画された。ショールーム内には、商品である車の展示スペースの他、日産の歴史を見せるギャラリースペース、関連グッズを販売するブティック、カフェが併設されている。日産のギャラリーの一貫したコンセプトである「日産が日本の企業であることをDNAレベルで伝える空間」という考えをもとに施設全体がデザインされている。

展示スペースの中央にある幅40mの壁面には、LEDが組み込まれ、壁面全体が映像ディスプレイとして機能し、建築内を2階レベルで通過する半公共の歩道へ向けてアピールしている。また、施設内には各所にオリジナルの家具が置かれ、車目的のお客に限らず、周辺地域からの来館者がくつろげるつくりになっている。大空間ながら、建築的な設備類を見せない工夫や外部からの施設の見え方、人々の動線計画など、あらゆる部分に細やかなインテリアデザインがなされている。

このデザインコンセプトは、「日産銀座ギャラリー」「本社ギャラリー（旧）」から継承されている。

銀座ギャラリーと本社ギャラリー（旧）は、東京銀座の最もにぎわう一等地にあり、日産の新しいブランドアイデンティティーを示す場として2001年に改装された。

銀座ギャラリーのエントランスは、塗装されたアルミ製のリブ形状ルーバーで覆われ、リブの水平方向への流れによって内部へ導くような印象を持たせ、同時に外部に対してシンボリックな表情を見せている。

1階は展示ルームになっており、車と空間を、「宝石とショーケース」の関係に見立てたつくりになっている。展示ルームの床壁を曲面でつなぎ、輪郭線をなくすことで、広くはない空間の距離感を曖昧にし、また、すべてをステンレスのバイブレーション仕上げにすることで車への映り込みを減らすなど、車を魅力的に見せるためのデザインがなされた。

2階はコーポレートコーナーとして、情報端末などで来訪者が日産のことを知ることができる場としてつくられた。

一方、本社ギャラリー（旧）は、ビルのメーンエントランスも兼ねるスペースとして計画された。インテリアの壁面には、アクリル樹脂系人工大理石のパネルが用いられている。パネルは薄くした切削部と開口部が反復し、そこに光を透過させることで、独特の光の濃淡を生んでいる。この素材と手法は、銀座ギャラリーにも一部用いられ、両ギャラリーに共通性を持たせたものである。また、躯体柱には、エンボスパターンをヒートプレスしたPVC樹脂パネルが貼られており、人工大理石とあわせ、単調な素材にさまざまな表情を持たせることで、さまざまな解釈の可能性を求めるデザインがなされた。

銀座でのボキャブラリーは、その後計画された「名古屋ギャラリー」「福岡ギャラリー」にも継承されている。

一方、札幌ギャラリーでは、銀座ギャラリーのデザインから継承する部分と、新たな視点が取り込まれている。既存としてある建築の内外部を一つの大きなボリュームとして捉え、建築を生かしながら外部からの車の見せ方などを考慮したデザインがなされている。継承する部分では、白い水平方向のアルミリブ材を用いながら、一部ではサイズを大きくするなど、素材と光の関係について発展させた使われ方をしている。また、ミラーへの映り込みや、人によって変化する光と影など、車と空間の関係を、ショーケース的な考え方から、見る人を介在させる展示へシフトチェンジしている。

NISSAN GALLERY GINZA

NISSAN GALLERY HEADQUARTERS (old)

NISSAN GALLERY SAPPORO

P6
Showroom
NISSAN GALLERY GLOBAL HEADQUARTERS
Minatomirai, Yokohama

P22
Showroom
NISSAN GALLERY GINZA
Ginza, Tokyo

P36
Showroom
NISSAN GALLERY HEADQUARTERS (old)
Ginza, Tokyo

P42
Showroom
NISSAN GALLERY SAPPORO
Sapporo, Hokkaido

The Nissan Global Headquarters Gallery was planned to be ancillary to the company headquarters when it was moved from Ginza, Tokyo, to Minatomirai, Yokohama, in 2009. In addition to display space for the company automobiles, the gallery contains gallery space to show Nissan's history, a boutique that sells related goods, and a cafe. The entire Nissan gallery facility was designed based on the unifying concept of "a space that conveys at the DNA level the fact that Nissan is a Japanese company." LEDs embedded into a 40-meter-wide wall in the center of the display space function as a video display aimed at a semipublic walkway that passes through the building at the second-floor level. The gallery is filled with original furniture to create a place where not only car buyers, but also visitors from the surrounding area can come to relax. While it is a large space, the interior was designed with attention to such details as tricks to hide architectural devices, the exterior view and people's line of sight.

This design concept was inherited from the Nissan Ginza Gallery and the former Headquarters Gallery. The Ginza Gallery and former Headquarters Gallery are in the best, most bustling part of Tokyo's Ginza district, and they were remodeled in 2001 to express Nissan's new grand identity. The Ginza Gallery entrance is covered in rib-shaped louvers of painted aluminum whose horizontal direction seems to guide visitors inside while serving a symbolic function when viewed from outside. The first floor is the display room, and it was designed to liken the cars and their surrounding space to jewels in a showcase. Curves connect the display room's floor and walls, eliminating boundary lines and making vague the distances in this small space; and the walls and floor are entirely made of stainless steel with a vibration finish, reducing their reflections in the cars to make the cars look more appealing. The second floor is the "corporate corner," created as a place where visitors can use terminals and other amenities to learn more about Nissan.

Meanwhile, the former Headquarters Gallery was designed to incorporate the entrance to the building. The walls of the interior use acrylic-resin-artificial-marble panels. The panels contain a pattern of alternating thin machined parts and openings into which light is shone to create a characteristic shade. These materials and this technique are also used in the Ginza gallery, giving the two galleries some commonality. Also, PVC resin panels with a heat-pressed embossed pattern are used in the skeletal pillars; combined with the artificial marble, these panels give a variety of appearances to monotonous materials and create a design open to a variety of interpretations.

The vocabulary of the Ginza Gallery was also inherited by the later Nagoya and Fukuoka galleries. By homogenizing the spacial elements of floor, walls and ceiling and by making the top and bottom of the space symmetrical, a design was achieved that blurs the concepts of above and below.

Meanwhile, the Sapporo Gallery has elements inherited from the galleries from Ginza to Nagoya, while also incorporating some new points of view. By thinking of the interior and exterior of the existing building as one big volume, Fumita achieved a design that makes the most of the architecture while taking into consideration such things as the appearance of the cars from outside. As for the inherited elements, the building uses white, horizontal aluminum ribs - enlarged in one section - to develop the relationship between the material and light. But with mirror reflections, light and shadows that change with people's actions and the idea of the cars and the space as a showcase, there is a shift to interposing the viewer into the display.

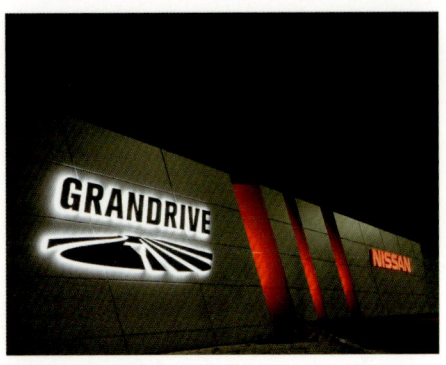

NISSAN GRANDRIVE

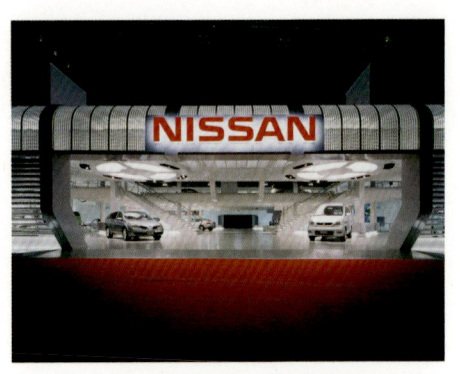

THE 35TH TOKYO MOTOR SHOW NISSAN BOOTH

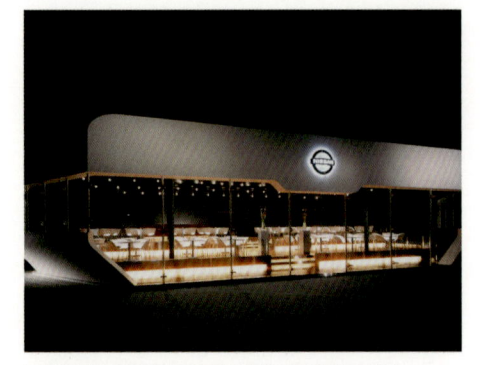

THE 36TH TOKYO MOTOR SHOW NISSAN BOOTH

P48
Guest Hall
NISSAN GRANDRIVE
Yokosuka, Kanagawa
日産グランドライブ

P54
Motorshow Booth
THE 35 TH TOKYO MOTOR SHOW
NISSAN BOOTH
Makuhari, Chiba
第35回東京モーターショー
日産ブース

P62
Motorshow Booth
THE 36 TH TOKYO MOTOR SHOW
NISSAN BOOTH
Makuhari, Chiba
第36回東京モーターショー
日産ブース

P66
Motorshow Booth
THE 37 TH TOKYO MOTOR SHOW
NISSAN BOOTH
Makuhari, Chiba
第37回東京モーターショー
日産ブース

この施設は、日産自動車の車を試走できるコースなどを備えた、試乗体験施設である。そのメーンゲート＆ゲストハウスを文田がデザインした。クライアントが求める「パッション」というキーワードから、この施設を訪れる顧客に対し、車に乗ることの楽しさや喜びを感じさせる施設が計画されている。「パッション」というキーワードと車の速度を表すものとして、オリジナルで調合された赤色が採用された。また、斜めになった建築の表情もパッションや速度、動的な感情を表している。施設内には、イベントホールやプレゼンテーションルーム、車が展示されたエキシビションルームなどがあり、車を介した新しいコミュニケーションスペースとしてつくられた。

2001年の「銀座ギャラリー」「本社ギャラリー（旧）」と同時期に、日産自動車のブランドアイデンティティーを発表する場として、モーターショーでのブースがつくられた。会場の風景にブースのデザインが溶け込んでしまわぬよう、モーターショーブースでは一般的にはタブーとされていた、壁や天井が制作されている。外部からの見えにくさを解消するため、パンチングメタルやルーバーが用いられ、空間を仕切りながらも、ショーブースとして機能している。ブース内には、アッパーデッキや天井の開口部が設けられ、また階段から車や車を俯瞰することもでき、変化に富んだ空間が実現された。

前回のモーターショーが一般ユーザー向けだったのに対し、この会場ではビジネス向けの商用車をメーンに開催された。そのため実利性重視で規模、予算とも縮小された条件でのデザインがなされている。デザイン要素として、白い壁面、エンボス、アール形状のコーナーなどがあり、またブースを完全に遮断することなく、視線の通るつくりでありながら、ブースに踏み入れると、日産の区画であることを意識できるよう計画された。ブースは、車の展示スペース、ステージのほか、商談・接待用のラウンジスペースで構成される。ガラスで外部と仕切られたラウンジは、テーブル席を設け、床を木調にし、顧客をもてなす空間として演出されている。

第35回の一般ユーザー向けのショーにて、壁面でブースを囲み、展示車をより際立たせた手法を継承しながら、第37回ではそこに音響、映像、照明の要素を加え、新たなプレゼンテーション空間がつくられた。展示スペースの周りを囲むように流れる映像ディスプレイには、日産の歴史や車種が流れ、それに連動し空間の照明が色を変える。より体感型、劇場型のブースがデザインされた。

THE 37TH TOKYO MOTOR SHOW NISSAN BOOTH

P48
Guest Hall
NISSAN GRANDRIVE
Yokosuka, Kanagawa

P54
Motorshow Booth
THE 35TH TOKYO MOTOR SHOW NISSAN BOOTH
Makuhari, Chiba

P62
Motorshow Booth
THE 36TH TOKYO MOTOR SHOW NISSAN BOOTH
Makuhari, Chiba

P66
Motorshow Booth
THE 37TH TOKYO MOTOR SHOW NISSAN BOOTH
Makuhari, Chiba

This is a test-drive facility for Nissan Motors automobiles. Fumita designed the main gate and guest house. Based on the keyword "passion," which was requested by the client, this facility was designed to let visitors feel the fun and joy of driving a car. To express the keyword "passion" and the speed of a car, an original-mixture red was used in the design. The appearance of the slanted building also expresses passion, speed and kinetic emotion. Inside the facility are an event hall, a presentation room and an automobile-exhibition room, creating a new space where communication is achieved through cars.

In 2001, along with the Ginza Gallery and the former Headquarters Gallery, a booth was created, at the Tokyo Motor Show, to announce the brand identity of Nissan Motors. So that the design of the booth would not fade into the scenery of the hall, walls and a ceiling - generally considered taboo for a motor show booth - were created. Punched metal and louvers were used to increase the booth's exterior visibility, and they served to both partition the space and function as a showcase. Inside the booth, openings were created for the upper deck and ceiling, and the stairs afforded a commanding view of the cars, achieving a space rich in variation.

In contrast with the prior Tokyo Motor Show, which was oriented toward the average car consumer, at this show, the focus was on companies' business fleets. So Nissan's display was designed with an emphasis on utility and with a reduced scale and budget. The design elements included white walls, embossing and curved corners, and while the booth was not completely closed off and allowed people to see inside, it was designed so that when a person set foot inside, he was aware that he was in the Nissan area. In addition to the car-exhibition space and the stage, the booth included a lounge space for business discussions and entertaining guests. This lounge, which was partitioned off from its exterior by glass, had table seating and a wood floor and was created as a space to make customers feel welcome.

For the 37th Tokyo Motor Show, the designer took from the booth of the 35th Tokyo Motor Show (which was oriented toward the average car consumer) the technique of enclosing the booth in walls to further highlight the cars on display. But this design added the elements of sound, images and lighting to create a new presentation space. The image display that flowed around the exhibit space as if to enclose it included scenes from Nissan's history and images of car models, and the lights changed in with the display. This booth design was more experiential and theatrical.

NATURAL BODY NAMBA CITY

NATURAL BODY KOBE INTERNATIONAL HOUSE SOL

NATURAL BODY SHIBUYA PARCO PART 3

P72
Hand Relaxation
NATURAL BODY NAMBA CITY
Namba, Osaka
ナチュラルボディ　なんばCITY店

P74
Hand Relaxation
NATURAL BODY
KOBE INTERNATIONAL HOUSE SOL
Chuo-ku, Kobe
ナチュラルボディ　神戸国際会館SOL店

P76
Hand Relaxation
NATURAL BODY
SHIBUYA PARCO PART 3
Shibuya, Tokyo
ナチュラルボディ　渋谷PARCO PART 3店

P80
Hand Relaxation
NATURAL BODY
HANKYU INTERNATIONAL
Chayamachi, Osaka
ナチュラルボディ　阪急インターナショナル店

ハンドリラクセーション「ナチュラルボディ」のいくつかの店舗をデザインする中で、文田はそのリラクセーション空間のためにいくつかの実験的な試みを行ってきた。一貫しているのは、直接光を極力なくし、間接光または透過光で空間全体を囲み込むこと。その空間のために、床、壁、天井、什器、家具といったエレメントの意味、既成概念を取り払い、光のための抽象的な装置として扱ってきた。また、空間コンセプトに合わせたマッサージチェアやベ

ッドなど、オリジナルで製作、改良が重ねられた。

大阪・難波にある複合商業施設内の「なんばシティ店」、同時期に計画された「神戸国際会館SOL店」では、天井から壁面に掛けてプラスターボードを曲げ加工した曲面でつながっており、特異な空間の距離感を感じさせ非日常空間を演出している。壁面の同系色によるストライプの塗装も距離感を強調する要素として計画されている。また、リラックスするための空間として、天井や壁面の穴から、ろうそくの火をイメージした柔らかい光がプレーンな空間に配灯されている。

「ナチュラルボディ 阪急インターナショナル店」では、天井全体が波打つような曲面になっている。間接光を生かすつくりであると共に、その内部には空調設備が隠されており、空間を演出する造形的な目的と機能が両立されている。また、ルーバー付きの壁面は、外部への開口部に向けて、光が漏れ、内部の雰囲気を伝えるスクリーンとなっている。

一方、「ナチュラルボディ 渋谷PARCO PART3店」では、新たな色の要素が取り込まれている。他店舗同様、マッサージチェアのシンボ

リックな形態と間接照明による柔らかい陰影の空間というコンセプトは守りながら、商品として販売されるミネラルウオーターをモチーフに、グラフィック的要素が展開された。パッケージのブルーを光り壁にボーダーラインとして用い、店内に展開されている。

P84
Boutique
M,I,D, SHOP UMEDA HANKYU
Umeda, Osaka
エム・アイ・ディー ショップ　阪急うめだ店

P88
Boutique
M,I,D, SHOP YURAKUCHO HANKYU
Yurakucho, Tokyo
エム・アイ・ディー ショップ　有楽町阪急店

P98
Boutique
M-PREMIER SHIJOKAWARAMACHI
HANKYU STORE
Shijokawaramachi, Kyoto
エム・プルミエ　四条河原町阪急店

P100
Boutique
M-PREMIER TENMAYA HIROSHIMA
HACCHOBORI STORE
Naka-ku, Hiroshima
エム・プルミエ　天満屋広島八丁堀店

アパレルメーカー「エム・アイ・ディー」には、複数のショップ形態がある。その中核をなす「エム・プルミエ」のデザインの大きなテーマは透過光である。人工大理石を切削し、光を透過させることでできる濃淡が、床、壁、天井のエレメントとして多用されている。「エム・プルミエ 四条河原町阪急店」では、その光の表情と白い床・壁、ステンレスといった素材が対比するように構成されている。一方、「エム・プルミエ 天満屋広島八丁堀店」では、店内全体にランダ

NATURAL BODY HANKYU INTERNATIONAL

M,I,D, SHOP UMEDA HANKYU

M,I,D, SHOP YURAKUCHO HANKYU

P72
Hand Relaxation
NATURAL BODY NAMBA CITY
Namba, Osaka

P74
Hand Relaxation
NATURAL BODY KOBE INTERNATIONAL HOUSE SOL
Chuo-ku, Kobe

P76
Hand Relaxation
NATURAL BODY SHIBUYA PARCO PART 3
Shibuya, Tokyo

P80
Hand Relaxation
NATURAL BODY HANKYU INTERNATIONAL
Chayamachi, Osaka

In designing a number of stores for the massage company "Natural Body," Fumita conducted several experiments in the creation of relaxation spaces. The consistent element was the elimination of as much direct light as possible and enveloping the entire space in indirect or transmitted light. For those spaces, he got rid of the meanings and preconceived notions of such elements as floors, walls, ceilings, fittings and furniture and treated them as abstract devices that serve the purposes of light. He made a number of original designs of and improvements on such items as massage chairs and beds to fit the interior concept.

For the "Nanba City Store," in a commercial complex in Osaka Nanba, and the "Kobe International House SOL Store," which was built at the same time, everything from the ceilings to the walls was connected with curved processed plasterboard to produce an out-of-the-ordinary space that conveys a singular sense of distance. Similarly colored stripes painted on the walls were designed as another element to emphasize the sense of distance. And because it was a space for relaxation, soft lights designed like candle flames were placed to shine through holes in the ceilings and walls and distribute light within the plain space.

In the "Natural Body Hankyu International Shop," the entire ceiling is covered in wavelike curves. The ceiling is designed to make good use of indirect light and also has air conditioning equipment hidden inside it, achieving both the artistic objectives of the design and functionality. Light leaks outside through apertures in the louver-equipped walls, creating a screen that conveys the ambiance of the interior.

Meanwhile, the "Natural Body Shibuya Parco Part 3 Store" incorporates new colors. It maintains the concept of the other stores of a space of soft shadows created by the symbolic shape of the massage chairs and indirect lighting, but develops graphical elements with a motif of the mineral water on sale in the store. The blue of the package is used as a borderline in lighted walls inside the store.

P84
Boutique
M,I,D, SHOP UMEDA HANKYU
Umeda, Osaka

P88
Boutique
M,I,D, SHOP YURAKUCHO HANKYU
Yurakucho, Tokyo

P98
Boutique
M-PREMIER SHIJOKAWARAMACHI HANKYU STORE
Shimogyo-ku, Kyoto

P100
Boutique
M-PREMIER TENMAYA HIROSHIMA HACCHOBORI STORE
Naka-ku, Hiroshima

The apparel maker M,I,D, has several different shop types. A big theme of the design of the core of them, the M-Premier stores, is transmitted light. The light and shade created by cutting artificial marble and transmitting light through it is used abundantly in the floor, wall and ceiling elements. In the M-Premier Shijo Kawaramachi Hankyu Store, stainless steel is used to contrast with that light and shade, and with the white of the floor and walls.
Meanwhile, random stripes are used throughout the interior of the M-Premier Tenmaya Hacchobori Hankyu Store. White

M-PREMIER SHIJOKAWARAMACHI HANKYU STORE 　　**M-PREMIER TENMAYA HIROSHIMA HACCHOBORI STORE** 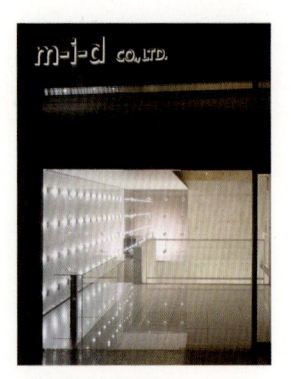　　**M,I,D, PRESS ROOM**

ムストライプが用いられている。壁面やパーティションに、白いストライプがランダムに並び、ガラスの透明な部分や鏡面部分と重なりながら、姿見や仕切りといった機能も包含したパターンがつくり上げられている。また、「エム・プルミエ」での透過光のディテールは、エム・アイ・ディーのブランドの他店舗で展開され、新たな形態が生み出されている。「エム・アイ・ディーショップ 阪急うめだ店」「同・有楽町阪急店」」では、その透過光のディテールが、塩ビの透明なブロックによってつくり上げられている。玩具としてつくられたクリアブロックを積層し、内照式の光り壁をつくり、壁内部の反射板で乱反射させることで雲模様のような光の表情を生んでいる。

P90
Pressroom
M,I,D, PRESS ROOM
Omotesando, Tokyo
エム・アイ・ディー プレスルーム

展示スペースとオフィスを有する、プレスルームとして、東京・表参道に計画された。既存ビルの1階と地下1階に、柱、壁など主要構造物にはほぼ手を加えず、デザインがなされている。コンクリート打ち放しの壁面は、透明ガラスを二重構造にしたボックスで覆われ、その中にオリジナルの照明器具が約400個取り付けられている。グリッド状に配置された照明器具のパターンが、ガラス壁面や床に反射、増幅し空間全体に広がる。この照明器具は鋳造したステンレスを更に加工したもので、遠景では曖昧に見える照明だが、近くで見ると強い実在感があり、この二面性が空間の全体から細部までをよりデザイン性の高いものとしている。

P94
Office
M,I,D, HEADQUARTERS
Honmachi, Osaka
エム・アイ・ディー 本社

P96
Office
M,I,D, HEADQUARTERS ANNEX
Honmachi, Osaka
エム・アイ・ディー 本社アネックス

アパレルメーカー「エム・アイ・ディー」の本社として機能するオフィスとビル1階にプレスルームがつくられた。バニッシングポイント(視界の中心)のレベルで上下シンメトリーに空間が構成されている。壁面に等間隔に並ぶ円柱状の照明をはじめ、天井と床に同じレイアウトでステンレスを施すなど、上下概念に問いかけるような空間が試みられている。
また、同時期に別館「エム・アイ・ディー 本社アネックス」の外装もデザインされた。建築をアルミルーバーのみで覆うつくりになっており、ルーバーの奥行き、ピッチをに変化がつけられている。ビルの前を通る人の視点の移動で、線状や立体的な表情が移り変わるよう構成されている。

P102
Boutique
TRE PINI
Nishi-ku, Kobe
トレピニ

このブティックでは、フレキシブルに設置場所を変えることのできる什器に加え、通常の物販店としての機能のほかに、カルチャースクールなどのイベントに使用できるスペースになることも求められたという。店内壁面には水平方向のルーバーが巡り、そのスリットにパーツを差し込むことで什器となるデザインである。スリットに差し込むパーツはルーバー内に収納することが可能である。イベント時には、棚什器と一体となったファサード壁面を移動させ、動線を変化させることができる。
機能的な壁面ルーバーであるが、床、天井との設置部分において、照明を仕込むことにより、スリットから光が透過し、その存在が曖昧に感じられるよう計画されている。

M,I,D, HEADQUARTERS    **M,I,D, HEADQUARTERS ANNEX**    **TRE PINI**

stripes are lined up randomly on the walls and partitions so as to overlap the transparent parts of the glass and the mirrors, creating a pattern that includes the functions of both full-length mirrors and partitions.

The detail of transmitted light used in the M-Premier stores has been further developed in the other shops of the M,I,D, brand, creating new forms. In M,I,D, Shop Umeda Hankyu Flagship Store and M,I,D, Shop Yurakucho Hankyu, the detail of transmitted light is created using translucent polyvinyl chloride blocks. Layering clear blocks created as toys to make internally illuminated walls and using reflective boards to diffusely reflect that light inside those walls gives rise to a cloud pattern of light.

P90
Pressroom
M,I,D, PRESS ROOM
Omotesando, Tokyo

The M,I,D, Press Room was designed in Omotesando, Tokyo, as a press room that would incorporate both exhibition space and office space. The design left almost untouched the main structures of the first floor and of the first underground floor of the existing building - such as the pillars and walls. Architectural-concrete walls were placed inside a box of double-paned, transparent glass, and 400 original light fixtures were installed inside. The grid pattern of the light fixtures is reflected in the glass walls and floor, amplifying it throughout the space. These light fixtures are made of cast stainless steel that underwent further processing; from a distance they have a vague appearance, but up close, they have a strong substantiality, and this duality increases the quality of the design both overall and down to the level of detail.

P94
Office
M,I,D, HEADQUARTERS
Honmachi, Osaka

P96
Office
M,I,D, HEADQUARTERS ANNEX
Honmachi, Osaka

The M,I,D, Press room was created on the first floor of an office building that serves as the headquarters of apparel maker M,I,D,. The space is composed so as to achieve symmetry of top and bottom at the vanishing-point level. Starting with evenly spaced, cylindrical lights on the walls and including stainless steel with the same layout on the ceiling and floor, it is an attempt to create a space that questions the concepts of above and below.

The exterior of the separate M,I,D, Headquarters Annex was designed in the same period of time. The building is covered only in aluminum louvers, with variation given to their depth and pitch. It is composed such that as the visual point of people passing in front of the building changes, the building's linear and three-dimensional appearances change.

P102
Boutique
TRE PINI
Nishi-ku, Kobe

This store was designed to have movable fittings so it would be usable as a space for culture school events and the like, in addition to functioning as a regular retail store. Horizontal louvers on the walls surround the space, and they were designed to allow fittings to be added by inserting parts into the louvers' slits. The parts inserted into the louvers can also be stowed away inside them. When there is an event, the store's traffic lines can be changed by moving facade walls that have built-in shelf fittings.

The wall louvers are functional, but when the ceiling and floor sections of them are fitted with lights, light passes through the slits, making visitors vaguely aware of the louvers' existence.

183

ETE AOYAMA

ETE+ NAGOYA LACHIC

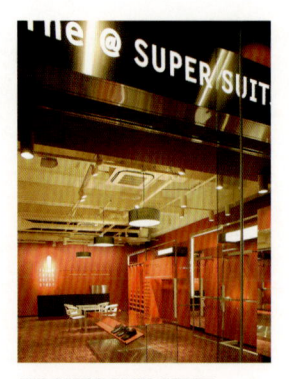

THE SUPER SUITS STORE AWAJICHO

P104
Accessory Shop
ETE AOYAMA
Minamiaoyama, Tokyo
エテ 青山本店

P106
Accessory Shop
ETE+ NAGOYA LACHIC
Nagoya, Aichi
エテ・プラス 名古屋ラシック店

ジュエリーやファッション雑貨を扱うショップ。このブランドの店舗づくりでは一貫して、空間の床、壁、天井などのボリュームが素材や光によって調節されている。
「エテ 青山店」では、間接光を用い、それぞれの面を明確にし、色と仕上げ材の違いによってその要素を際立たせている。
「エテ・プラス 名古屋ラシック」では、間接光のほか木質素材、ステンレススチール、透明ガラスを用い、壁面や置き什器のボリューム操作が行われている。

P108
Boutique
THE SUPER SUITS STORE AWAJICHO
Awajicho, Tokyo
ザ・スーパースーツストア 淡路町店

「ザ・スーパースーツストア」は、2種の固定価格で営業するスーツショップである。ブランドとしてのコンセプトは、身長、体格のサイズごとに整理し配置することで、必要なものを見つけやすくすること。そのため、以前の什器は目立たせないよう白く軽量感のあるデザインであった。リニューアルによって、整理して見せるというコンセプトはそのままに、什器はスーツを抱え込む形とし、スーツの背景が上質なものとなるよう、空間の密度感や重量感を与える"赤"を用いたデザインが試みられた。合わせて、店全体には質感の感じられるカーペットが敷かれた。什器は、商品の整理、什器としての機能のほか、商品が並んだ際の見え方はグラフィックデザイナーの視点からも考えられている。

P110
Boutique & Common Space
OSAKA TAKASHIMAYA ROOM IN BLOOM
Namba, Osaka
ルームインブルーム 大阪高島屋

百貨店・大阪高島屋でのフロアリニューアルに伴い、物販店を含む共用部と独立した3店舗をデザイン。共用部に各店舗のアイデンティティーが乱立しないよう、各店舗、クライアントと全体の有機的なつながりと調和をコンセプトにフロア設計された。区画割りも共用部と店舗を明確に分けず、空気感を共有する、大きなゾーンの各パートとして考えられたつくりになっている。

P114
Showroom
SPIRITUAL MODE MINAMIAOYAMA
Minamiaoyama, Tokyo
スピリチュアルモード 南青山

P122
Showroom
SPIRITUAL MODE KYOTO
Kamitoba, Kyoto
スピリチュアルモード 京都

「スピリチュアルモード」はシステムバスを中心とした住宅設備メーカーのショールームである。文田のデザインした同社のバスタブやその付属機器を販売し、空間デザインでブランドのイメージを示すことができる施設づくりが求められた。
「南青山店」では、アプローチから店内にかけて、スピリチュアルモードのロゴの形や、ヘキサゴン(六角形)をモチーフにした、ステンレスと光を使った壁面が構成されている。ヘキサゴンの完結した形やそれを分解した曖昧な形、光が、天井や壁面に反射し万華鏡のような効果をもたらしている。商品のバスタブを展示するだけでなく、周辺環境、機器のデザインも文田より総合的に提案され、また、商談スペースのテーブルやイスもオリジナルでデザインされている。バスタブが住空間の一部であるというブランドのメッ

OSAKA TAKASHIMAYA ROOM IN BLOOM

SPIRITUAL MODE MINAMIAOYAMA

SPIRITUAL MODE KYOTO

P104
Accessory Shop
ETE AOYAMA
Minamiaoyama, Tokyo

P106
Accessory Shop
ETE+ NAGOYA LACHIC
Nagoya, Aichi

Here are two shops that deal in various jewelry and fashion items. These shops' designs consistently control the space between the floor, walls and ceiling using raw materials and light.
In Ete Aoyama, each surface is made clearly visible using indirect lighting, and elements are made conspicuous via variations in color and finishing material.
At Ete + Nagoya Lachic, in addition to indirect lighting, wood material, stainless steel and transparent glass are used to manipulate the space around the walls and around the freestanding fittings.

P108
Boutique
THE SUPER SUITS STORE AWAJICHO
Awajicho, Tokyo

This is a suit shop that uses two types of fixed prices. The brand concept is arranging and placing suits by height and body type to make it easy for customers to find what they need. For this reason, the store had a light, white design to keep the existing fittings from standing out. Through the renovation, the concept of organizing and displaying was implemented by giving the fittings a shape that holds the suits, and using a red design that brings density and weight to space so that high-grade items could be placed in the suits' background. In keeping with this idea, high-grade carpet was placed throughout the interior. The fittings were designed to not just organize the products and serve the functions of fittings, but to display the products with a graphic designer's sensibilities.

P110
Boutique & Common Space
OSAKA TAKASHIMAYA ROOM IN BLOOM
Namba, Osaka

In conjunction with the renovation of a floor of the department store Osaka Takashimaya, Fumita designed three independent shops and a common area where goods are sold. So that the individual identities of each shop would not flood the common area, he consulted with each shop and client to design the floor based on the concepts of harmony and organically connecting the whole. In sectioning the space, he avoided clearly dividing the shared area and each store, and instead thought of them as parts of a large zone.

P114
Showroom
SPIRITUAL MODE MINAMIAOYAMA
Minamiaoyama, Tokyo

P122
Showroom
SPIRITUAL MODE KYOTO
Kamitoba, Kyoto

Spiritual Mode is the showroom of a household equipment maker that specializes in system baths. It sells bathtubs designed for the company by Fumita along with ancillary equipment, and the client requested for it a facility design that would express the brand's image. The Minami Aoyama store, from its approach to the interior, is composed of walls made using light and stainless steel in the shape of the spiritual Mode logo or with a hexagon motif. Complete hexagons and the vague shapes of disintegrating hexagons reflect off the ceiling and walls to create a kaleidoscopic effect. The space not only is used to exhibit bathtubs, it also generally suggests the designs of their ambient surroundings and equipment, and has a space for business discussions with originally designed tables and chairs. It is an interior design that

DCMX SITE 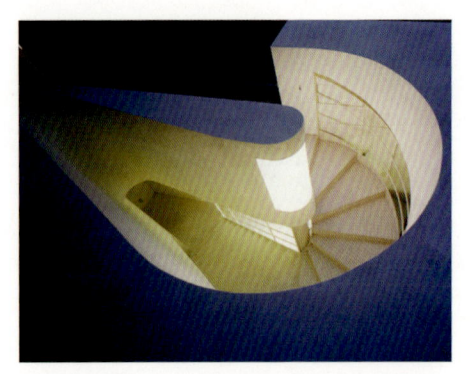 K-TWO UMEDA  K-TWO SHINSAIBASHI

セージをより伝える空間づくりがなされている。
「京都店」は、青山店の空間のアイデンティティーを継承しながら、新たなデザイン手法が試みられた。2層吹き抜けの展示スペースでは、ストライプパターンの成形ガラスが壁に用いられている。この抽象的なパターンが、見る人に「和」と「洋」、「古典」や「現代」、「未来」などを感じされるよう計画された。また、ファサードは、外部のさまざまな建築が並ぶ混沌とした環境に紛れてしまわぬよう、「図」として形を押し出すのではなく、建築全体を「地」として奥ゆかしい存在感を持つよう考え、白を多用したマッシブな外観となった。

P128
Showroom
DCMX SITE
Shinjuku, Tokyo
DCMX サイト

通信事業会社NTTドコモの携帯端末のショールーム。銀行とのコラボレーションで計画され、ATMや携帯端末の展示スペースや、イベントスペースがある。
店内は、さまざまな情報発信のスペースをイメージし、天井から壁面にかけて、ステンレスや木などを用い、さまざまな形状の面が構成されている。また、携帯端末をプロダクトデザインとして見せるためのオリジナル展示什器は、静態展示のものと手にとって試す動態展示のタイプがある。半円柱のケースを回転させるタイプと、光るボックスにステンレスの柱が並ぶ置き什器があり、これは、内照式の人工大理石の下から端末に伸びるコードを内包する機能を持っている。

P132
Hair Salon
K-TWO UMEDA
Umeda, Osaka
ケイ・ツー　梅田店

この美容室は、大阪・梅田の駅前の地下に立地しており、通常のサインでは街の風景に埋もれてしまう可能性があったため、「主張しないことで、その存在感が際立つようなファサード」のデザインが試みられた。地下への入り口に白い塊をつくり、そこをヘアピンカーブ状にくり抜いたようなアプローチを設けている。階段を下りると、シリンダー状の天井と壁面を持つ内部空間がつくられている。この恣意的な形状は、店舗区画の形状や構造梁を考慮した上での造形で、カットスペースとシャンプースペースのパーティションも兼ねている。

P134
Hair Salon
K-TWO SHINSAIBASHI
Shinsaibashi, Osaka
ケイ・ツー　心斎橋店

この美容室は、ビルの2階に位置し、幅広いガラスの開口部を有している。その開口部から外部へ店の存在をアピールするため、120本の照明器具が設置された店内の天井を見せている。1本の照明器具には2本のFL管が内蔵され、円筒状の乳半アクリルで包んでいる。スタイリングスペースは白を基調にデザインされ、待合スペースは「ギャラリー」にしたいというクライアントの要望でOSB板を黒染色して用いられている。空間が白と木調によってゾーニングされ、クールさと温かみがある店舗が演出されている。

communicates the brand message that the bathtub is part of the living space.

The Kyoto shop inherits the interior-design identity of the Aoyama shop while also experimenting with new design techniques. Striped-pattern glass is used in the walls of the two-floor-well exhibition space. This abstract pattern is designed to give the viewer a sense of freedom with regard to geography and time. And so that the facade doesn't slip into the chaos of the various buildings outside, a massive exterior was created using an abundance of white to present the building as "ground" rather than pushing out its shape as "figure."

P128
Showroom
DCMX SITE
Shinjuku, Tokyo

This is the cell phone showroom of communications company NTT docomo. Planned as a collaboration with banks, it has exhibition space for ATMs and cell phones, as well as event space.

Based on the image of a space for information transmission of all kinds, variously shaped surfaces were put together using stainless steel and wood to be placed everywhere from the ceiling to the walls. For originally designed display fixtures to show off the product design of the cell phones, static displays were used hand in hand with dynamic displays. There is a revolving half-column case type as well as a freestanding fixture type in which stainless-steel pillars are lined up in lighted boxes. These can contain cords stretching from the bottom of the internally lit artificial marble up to the cell phones.

P132
Hair Salon
K-TWO UMEDA
Umeda, Osaka

This beauty parlor is located underground in front of Osaka's Umeda Station, and because it was possible that a normal sign would be obscured by the scenery, the designer attempted to create "a facade that is conspicuous by virtue of not trying to stand out." A white mass was created at the entrance underground, and a hairpin-curve-shaped approach leading down was created as if excavated out of that mass. Down the stairs is an interior space with cylindrical ceiling and walls. This arbitrary shape was modeled taking into account the shape of the store's boundaries and the structural beams, and it serves as a partition between the haircutting space and the shampoo space.

P134
Hair Salon
K-TWO SHINSAIBASHI
Shinsaibashi, Osaka

This beauty salon is on the second floor of a building and has a wide glass opening. To draw attention to the shop, the ceiling, which has 120 light fixtures on it, was made visible through that opening to people outside. One light fixture contains two fluorescent bulbs and is enclosed in a milky white acrylic cylinder. The hair-styling space has a design based primarily on the color white, and the waiting area uses black-stained oriented strand board to fulfill the client's request that it be a gallery. The interior is zoned using white and wood to produce a store with both coolness and warmth.

SALON

ANAYI SHINJUKU ISETAN

ANAYI HIROSHIMA FUKUYA EKIMAE

P138
Hair Salon
SALON
Ginza, Tokyo
サロン

P140
Boutique
ANAYI SHINJUKU ISETAN
Shinjuku, Tokyo
アナイ　新宿伊勢丹店

P142
Boutique
ANAYI HIROSHIMA FUKUYA EKIMAE
Minami-ku, Hiroshima
アナイ　福屋広島駅前店

P144
Boutique
ESSENCE OF ANAYI TOKYO MIDTOWN
Roppongi, Tokyo
エッセンス オブ アナイ　東京ミッドタウン店

P146
Boutique
ANAYI NISHINOMIYA HANKYU
Nishinomiya, Hyogo
アナイ　西宮阪急店

P148
Boutique
MANOUQUA SHIN MARUNOUCHI BUILDING
Marunouchi, Tokyo
マヌーカ　新丸ビル店

東京・銀座にあるヘアサロン。レセプションは、落ち着いた印象の木が用多く用いられている。そのレセプションからスタイリングスペースに続くアプローチを通り、扉をくぐると、白に包まれた空間が広がる。スタイリングスペースは、白を基調としたインテリアで、レセプションゾーンと対比的な空間がつくり上げられている。

2004年に新たにオープンした、ブティック「アナイ 新宿伊勢丹店」では、ブランドとしての新しいアイデンティティーを感じさせるデザインが求められた。そこで提案されたのが、木や暖色系の素材を用いた表現である。店内は、矩形やL字型という抽象的なパターンを重ねた面により構成されている。それぞれの素材に、木、電解着色したブロンズ色のアルミ、間接光を用いて3次元的なレイヤーが形づくられた。シンプルな形のパーツがスライドしたような壁面は、パターンが増殖していくような動きのある表現となっている。また、これら立体的な造形は、什器としての機能も含有している。そのほか置き什器は、壁面との違和感がないようシンプルなボックス形とし、ガラスの箱の中に木の箱が浮いて見えるつくりとなっている。
「福屋広島駅前店」「西宮阪急店」「エッセンス オブ アナイ 東京ミッドタウン店」では、新宿伊勢丹店から店づくりのテーマを継承し、同じく素材、色、光という素材が立体的なレイヤーとして構成され、また、物件ごとに異なる要素が組み込まれている。また「福屋広島駅前店」では、矩形面材が更に重層し、より立体的なつくりとなったのに対し、「西宮阪急店」「エッセンス オブ アナイ 東京ミッドタウン店」では、その面材とすき間の「図と地」の関係を反転させ、凸形立体の線がつくられた。

ブティック「アナイ」のアパレルメーカーによる別ブランドの店舗。店内壁面に大小の円形の穴を開け、構成されている。このブランドの、ビジュアルアイデンティティーの一つとしてデザインされた。

ESSENCE OF ANAYI TOKYO MIDTOWN

ANAYI NISHINOMIYA HANKYU

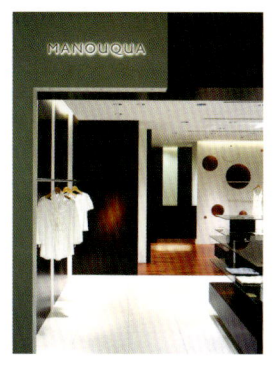

MANOUQUA SHIN MARUNOUCHI BUILDING

P138
Hair Salon
SALON
Ginza, Tokyo

This is a hair salon in Ginza, Tokyo. In the reception area, abundant use was made of wood that gives a calm impression. Passing through the approach way and a door to the styling space, visitors find a large area all covered in white. This styling area is white-based to contrast with the reception area.

P140
Boutique
ANAYI SHINJUKU ISETAN
Shinjuku, Tokyo

P142
Boutique
ANAYI HIROSHIMA FUKUYA EKIMAE
Minami-ku, Hiroshima

P144
Boutique
ESSENCE OF ANAYI TOKYO MIDTOWN
Roppongi, Tokyo

P146
Boutique
ANAYI NISHINOMIYA HANKYU
Nishinomiya, Hyogo

For the boutique Anayi Shinjuku Isetan, which opened in 2004, the client requested a design that would convey the brand's new identity. So a spatial expression was suggested that would use wood and warm colors. The interior was composed using surfaces that pile up abstract patterns of rectangles and letter Ls. Each article creates three-dimensional layers using wood, bronze-colored aluminum with electrolytically colored anodic oxide coating and indirect lighting. The walls, into which simply shaped parts are slid, express the motion of the patterns propagating. These three-dimensional creations also function as fittings. So that they would not seem out-of-place with the walls, the other, freestanding fittings were given simple box shapes, and they were made to look like wooden boxes are floating inside glass boxes.

Anayi Hiroshima Fukuya Ekimae, Anayi Nishinomiya Hankyu and Essence of Anayi Tokyo Midtown inherited the design theme of Anayi Shinjuku Isetan and were composed with the same three-dimensional layouts of color, light and materials, with different elements incorporated into each item.

While in the case of Anayi Hiroshima Fukuya Ekimae, rectangular surfaces are piled up even further to create more of a mass, at Anayi Nishinomiya Hankyu and Essence of Anayi Tokyo Midtown, space is opened up between those surfaces to reverse the relationship between "figure and ground" and create the lines of convex structures.

P148
Boutique
MANOUQUA SHIN MARUNOUCHI BUILDING
Marunouchi, Tokyo

This store is by the apparel maker behind the boutique "Anayi," but it has a separate brand. It has circular holes of various sizes on the walls inside. The shop was designed to represent one of the visual identities of the brand.

IXC COLLECTA TAMAGAWA TAKASHIMAYA

INHALE+ EXHALE KOBE FASHION MART

INHALE+EXHALE SHINKOBE ORIENTAL HOTEL

P150
Lifestyle Shop
IXC COLLECTA TAMAGAWA TAKASHIMAYA
Futakotamagawa, Tokyo
イクスシー コレクタ 玉川高島屋店

大型百貨店内のライフスタイルショップ。店舗区画の奥行きが、1.3mの狭いスペースで、壁面を生かしたデザインがなされている。商品は、衣類、テーブルウエア、バス用品、雑貨など複数のカテゴリーで構成されている。それらの商品を同じ壁面にディスプレイし、「フレーム」「壁面パネル」「可動棚」によってカテゴリーごとに領域が分けられている。各カテゴリーを木製フレームで囲いながら、壁面パネルは領域を越えて縦断、そこにフレキシブルに可動する棚が加わることで、重層的に商品がディスプレイされる。各カテゴリーが完全に分離することなく、緩やかにつながりながら、一つの絵のような表情を持った什器壁面がつくり上げられている。

P152
Boutique
INHALE+ EXHALE
KOBE FASHION MART
Higashinada-ku, Kobe
インヘイル＋エクスヘイル
神戸ファッションマート店

このブティックは、兵庫・神戸の複合文化施設にある。店の区画は、建築の構造柱によって四つに分断された、約30mの間口を持っており、その間口を重量感のあるデザインにつくり上げている。柱をまとめてOSB（オリエンテッド・スランド・ボード）で囲み、一つの塊として見せ、そこから削りだしたような開口部やディテールによって、抽象的かつ多義的な重量感ある塊のファサードが生み出されている。店内の壁面什器にもOSBを用い、塊感のある造形が施すと同時に、さまざまな商品ディスプレイに対応するシステムが組み込まれている。また、重量感のある壁面に対し、高い天井やステンレス製の置き什器が空間のバランスをとる役割を担っている。

P154
Boutique
INHALE+ EXHALE SHINKOBE ORIENTAL HOTEL
Chuo-ku, Kobe
インヘイル＋エクスヘイル
新神戸オリエンタルホテル店

開口部は高さ4mの天井面まであるガラス張りで、店内の印象が一目で見てとれるつくりになっている。店内の天井はシリンダーボールト形状になっており、切削感のある造形になっている。この天井の形状は、造形的要素だけでなく、照明や空調設備といった機能も一体化されており、古典的な印象を払拭する役割も含んでいるという。また、置きハンガーラックは、蛍光灯とアクリル板を組み合わせ、用途によって上下するラック部分のつくりなど、機能性とシステムを見せる形になっている。

P158
Office
FUMITA DESIGN OFFICE
Daikanyama, Tokyo
文田昭仁デザインオフィス

1970年代築のマンションのワンフロアに計画された自社オフィス。オフィスには不向きな散在する水回りを取り払い、空間を制限する壁式構造を逆手に取り造形化することで、単なる「壁」の意味を消去している。天井と壁、壁と床、壁と扉を同素材で構成し、自己完結した形状を持つプリミティブな空間がつくり上げられた。同時に扉などの機能（ヒンジ、ドアノブ）をなくし、よりエレメントとの融和するようデザインされている。そのほか、さまざまな色温度の照明を備えた会議室や実験室などがあり、空間におけるマテリアルの検証などクリエーティブオフィスとしての機能の充実が図られている。

FUMITA DESIGN OFFICE

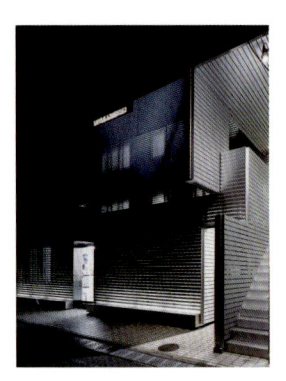

LITTLE ANDERSEN

P150
Lifestyle Shop
IXC COLLECTA
TAMAGAWA TAKASHIMAYA
Futakotamagawa, Tokyo

P152
Boutique
INHALE+ EXHALE
KOBE FASHION MART
Higashinada-ku, Kobe

P154
Boutique
INHALE + EXHALE SHINKOBE
ORIENTAL HOTEL
Chuo-ku, Kobe

P158
Office
FUMITA DESIGN OFFICE
Daikanyama, Tokyo

This is a lifestyle shop in a large department store. The shop's design makes good use of the walls within its mere 1.3-meters-long space. The products for sale are divided into categories including clothing, tableware, bath supplies and miscellaneous. The products are displayed on the same wall and divided by category using frames, wall panels and movable shelves. Each category is surrounded by a wooden frame and a wall panel cuts across the section's space; the addition of shelving that can be moved around easily allows products to be displayed in multiple layers. The categories are not completely partitioned off, but rather gently connected, creating furniture walls that present a single appearance like a picture.

This boutique is in a cultural complex in Kobe, Hyogo. The boutique is sectioned off by the building's structural pillars, which divide the space into four and provide about 30 meters of frontage, designed to have a sense of weight. The pillars are surrounded by oriented strand board to appear as one mass, and the opening and details - both of which look like they were carved out of that mass - create a facade with an abstract and ambiguous sense of weight. OSB was also used for the fixtures on the walls, creating moldings with substantiality and simultaneously creating a system compatible with the display of various merchandise. A high ceiling and stainless steel ornaments contrast with the weighty walls to achieve balance in the space.

The opening of this store has a glass wall that extends all the way to its 4-meter-high ceiling and allows viewers to get an impression of the interior at a glance. The interior has a cylindrical vaulted ceiling molded so as to feel like it was cut out. The ceiling's shape not only serves as a creative element, but also incorporates the functions of lighting and air conditioning, and eliminates any classical impression. The free-standing hanger racks, made of fluorescent lights and acrylic board, display both functionality and a systemic element with their rack section that can be raised and lowered depending on use.

This is Fumita's design-firm office, on a floor of an apartment building built in the 1970s. He removed the scattered parts of the building where water is circulated, such as the kitchen and bathroom, and turned the tables on the wall-style construction by making it part of the creative design and erasing the simple meaning of the word "wall." The ceiling, walls, floor and doors are all made of the same material, creating a primitive space with a self-contained shape. At the same time, the functions of doors (hinges, doorknobs) were eliminated to create a design more at harmony with the other elements. There are also a meeting room and a laboratory equipped with lights of various color temperatures so that the functions of a creative office, such as material inspection, can be amply carried out.

H-HOUSE

P162
Office Exterior
LITTLE ANDERSEN
Shibuya, Tokyo
リトルアンデルセン

鉄骨造の既存建築をアルミのルーバーで覆い、ピッチの疎密で表情に変化を生み、全体のボリュームを調整している。

P164
House
H-HOUSE
Shibuya, Tokyo
H邸

この住宅は、閑静な住宅街にある。建築内部への要求と外部からの制限の中で、必然的にできるボリュームを、可能な限りそのままのプリミティブな形態で実現することが試みられた。具体的な建材で実現していくにあたり、それらのディテールによって不要な意味を含まぬよう、ノイズを消去するためのディテールが施されている。また、内部においては、照明や空調などの設備を機能に支障のない限り隠蔽し、設備が形状を主張しないよう設えられている。そのほか、エレメント同士にクリアランスが設けられ空気の出入り口とするとともに、建築のボリュームを分割、自立させる造形的手法にもなっている。

P162
Office Exterior
LITTLE ANDERSEN
Shibuya, Tokyo

This is the exterior design of an apparel brand's offices. The existing steel frame of the building was covered in aluminum louvers, and by altering the pitch of the louvers, their appearance is changed, as is that of the whole building.

P164
House
H-HOUSE
Shibuya, Tokyo
H邸

This housing project is in a quiet residential neighborhood. Between the building's internal demands and external limitations, Fumita tried as much as possible to leave the space in its primitive original state. When it came time to achieve this using actual building materials, he tried to implement the details in a way that would cancel out all noise of extraneous meanings. Inside, equipment such as lights and air conditioning were hidden to the extent possible without hindering their functionality, while care was taken that such equipment not emphasize form over function. Also, clearance was created between elements and it was used to allow air to enter and exit, while the building's available space was divided up using creative methods to allow each home to be independent.